HOUSE STYLES AT A GLANCE

Best Wish
Marni Van Buren

AN ILLUSTRATED GUIDE

HOUSE STYLES AT A GLANCE

MAURIE VAN BUREN

LONGSTREET PRESS
Atlanta, Georgia

Published by
LONGSTREET PRESS, INC.
2150 Newmarket Parkway
Suite 102
Marietta, Georgia 30067

Printed in the United States of America

1st printing 1991

Library of Congress Catalog Card Number: 90-063900

ISBN 0-929264-85-1

This book was printed by R. R. Donnelley & Sons, Harrisonburg,
Virginia. The text was set in Century Schoolbook by
Typo-Repro Service, Inc., Atlanta, Georgia.
Illustrations by Richard Erickson and Jill Dible.
Text Design by Jill Dible.

Dedicated to the memory of
Hortense Golsen Richman

TABLE OF CONTENTS

INTRODUCTION

Homes can be read like a book, recounting stories of past and present. They vividly illustrate the age in which they were created, reflecting its technology, spirit, fashions, communications, materials, and climate. A home can depict the values, status, aspirations, and needs of the family it was built to shelter. Houses are not only a basic component of the American landscape and economy, they are the fundamental expression of the American dream. The more you know about them, the more interesting the houses in your community become. *House Styles at a Glance* was created to make it easy and fun to increase your knowledge and visual literacy.

Identifying styles is a way to classify houses into a pattern that is both interesting and meaningful. This pictorial guide will make it possible for you to identify and describe a wide range of house styles, whether you are a real estate professional or a person who simply enjoys looking at houses as a recreational pastime. The book has been designed to be easy to use and has several unique features.

This guide organizes house styles into commonly recognized categories (Traditional, Victorian, European, Contemporary, and Familiar American) for quick, easy reference. Most architectural style books are organized in chronological order, detailing the evolution of styles from Colonial times through World War II. While that structure makes it easy to illustrate how one style develops as a reaction against an earlier style, and how some styles jump back in time to revive a style popular several generations earlier, in order to use such a book as a reference you must first be familiar with the overall history of architecture to know where to find a particular style. Houses in the real world, however, are not organized chronologically.

Names of styles in this guide are simple and clear. Each style is named for its design elements rather than for its precise date of construction. Unfortunately, the difficult task of creating names for styles has been further complicated because of the pattern of copying earlier styles again and again. Architectural historians tack prefixes such as "Neo" or suffixes such as "Revival" onto styles in an attempt to impose some chronological order upon this pattern. The result is a purely academic nomenclature ("Neoclassical Revival," for example) which can become needlessly cumbersome and confusing. The art of devising names for styles is at best imprecise, and architectural historians are often in disagreement. For the purposes of this book, the guiding principle is that short, simple, descriptive names are more likely to be understood, used, and remembered.

This guide illustrates styles of houses being built today as well as those of yesteryear, thus providing insight into the relationship between the past and present. Background information on each style explains how it developed, and when and where the style was popular in America. Houses illustrated in this book do not represent landmarks in the history of architecture; there are already plenty of books on the market which fulfill that need. Instead, the illustrations depict the most common house styles, those you are likely to see in suburbs, small towns, rural areas, and cities. At the same time it attempts to illustrate the full gamut of house styles, from elegant mansions, to middle-class homes, to workers' cottages.

Identifying house styles depends on observing a wealth of information and pinpointing those features which fit into an established category. This pictorial guide to styles makes the task easy. Architectural details and terms are labeled directly on a line drawing of each house style. Under each drawing a concise paragraph entitled "At a Glance" lists the identifying features of the style. On the facing page is a "Focus on Features," where selected elements of the style are highlighted and explained in more detail. Anecdotes about the function or history of a particular element help you interpret the social history of the various styles. Knowledge of these details will help you understand, classify, and talk about houses like an architectural expert.

Let this book be your guide to a new visual literacy. It can serve as a basis for a lifetime of learning and give you a new appreciation for the houses you see every day.

TRADITIONAL

GEORGIAN

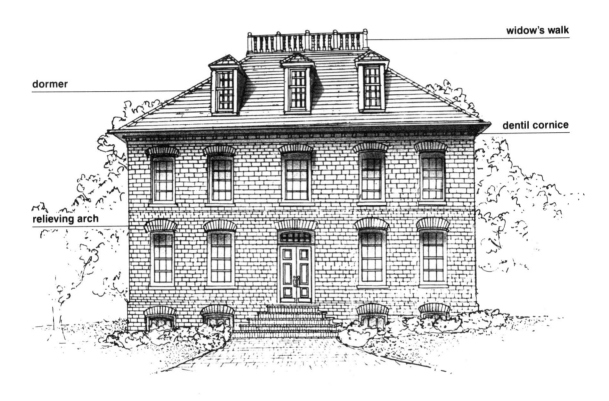

dormer

widow's walk

dentil cornice

relieving arch

At a Glance: The Georgian style is easily identified as a red brick box with symmetrically arranged windows, each having many small panes of glass. Georgian houses are usually capped with a hip or gable roof, and ornamentation is found around the door and at the cornice. Dormer windows are also common.

Background: The Georgian style gets its name from the several kings named George who ruled the British empire when America was still a colony. This style was imported from England, and original Georgian houses (i.e., dating from 1700 through the 1770s) exist only in the thirteen colonies. However, the re-creation of Williamsburg in the 1930s did more to promote the revival of the Georgian style than could have ever been imagined. Reproductions of Georgian houses patterned after Williamsburg soon began to line the streets of American neighborhoods, and they have continued to ever since. Millions of American tourists have visited Williamsburg to learn about life in a Colonial city, and as a result the Georgian Revival style is one of the most enduringly popular house styles in America.

Focus on Features

Dentil motif takes its name from *dent*, the Latin stem for tooth, and *motif* means repeating pattern. The *cornice* refers to the uppermost part of the wall. Thus, a dentil cornice consists of a running line of little blocks which project out like teeth. It is a very common classical molding, used both inside and out. This elegant design may have had a structural origin in the projecting ends of roof rafters found in ancient Greek temples.

A *widow's walk* is a boxed area on top of the roof with a balustrade railing. A *baluster* is a short, often round column which supports a handrail or coping. The term *balustrade* describes the complete system of all balusters and the top and bottom rails. According to legend, wives of seafaring captains could stand here to look over the seascape and search for the ship of their returning husbands. Often the husband did not return; hence the name widow's walk. Originally, the function of the widow's walk was to facilitate repair of the roof or chimney.

Windows provide a clue to the date of a house. This is a *double-hung sash window* which slides up and down within a frame. Each sash has six panes of glass, so it is called a *six-over-six* window. In earlier times glass had to be blown, giving it a waxy, often imperfect surface with tiny bubbles. Because of the limitations of early glass-making techniques, panes were small. The general rule is the more panes of glass in each sash, the earlier the date of the house.

PALLADIAN GEORGIAN

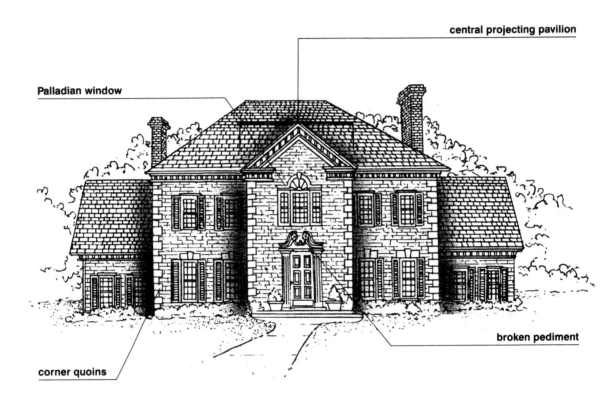

central projecting pavilion

Palladian window

corner quoins

broken pediment

At a Glance: Palladian Georgian houses are symmetrical brick buildings with a central projecting pavilion. Classical ornamenation is found around the door and at the cornice. Windows have small panes of glass and are often topped with lintels and a keystone. Palladian windows are especially common in twentieth-century Georgian Revivals. In general, Palladian Georgian houses are more formal and ornamental than the early Georgian style.

Background: Palladian Georgian is also referred to as the Late Georgian style because extant examples from the Colonial era were constructed after 1750. Georgian architects in England were greatly influenced by the buildings of the Italian Renaissance, especially by the work of Renaissance architect Andrea Palladio (1508-1580). A common feature of Palladio's designs adopted by this Georgian style was the central projecting pavilion. Although this style was rare in Colonial times, it was extremely popular in late-twentieth-century Georgian Revival homes throughout the country.

Focus on Features

The *pavilion* is the part of the building which projects out from the wall surface. (The term is also used to designate a detached building used for a special purpose such as entertaining.) A central projecting pavilion is a key feature of the Palladian Georgian style.

A *Palladian window* has three parts: a central arched portion flanked by tall, narrow sidelights. At first glance, Andrea Palladio, who began his career as a stonemason, seems an unlikely candidate for the architectural superstar status he has achieved. The fact is, however, that design ideas illustrated in his *The Four Books of Architecture* have been copied over and over again for the last four hundred years.

Inexpensive carpenters' handbooks available in the eighteenth century provided instructions for creating classical ornamentation. For example, this front door has a broken pediment—i.e., one which has been split apart at the center. The broken pediment has its origins in Roman and Baroque architecture and has long been popular in furniture design.

FEDERAL

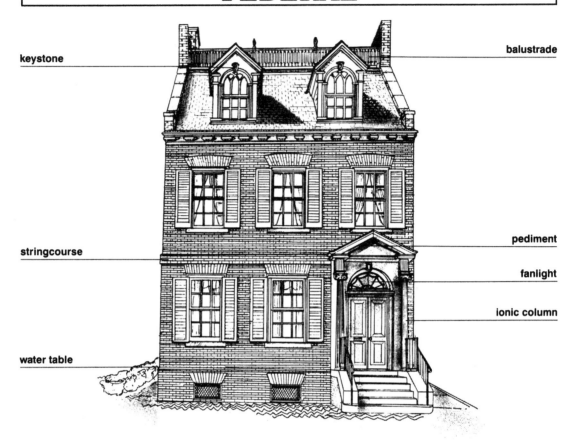

keystone

balustrade

stringcourse

pediment

fanlight

ionic column

water table

At a Glance: The hallmark of the Federal style is the fanlight, which arches delicately over the door like a spider's web. The original Federal houses were rectangular symmetrical buildings, two or three stories tall. The Federal interior often includes graceful classical swags and sunbursts on mantels and plaster—features of the Adam style, named for Scottish architect Robert Adam, who popularized this type of ornament.

Background: The Federal (or Adam) style was first popular in America shortly after the Revolutionary War. It was then that archeological excavations of the ancient Roman cities of Herculaneum and Pompeii created a fashion rage for ancient Roman culture and art. At the same time, Thomas Jefferson declared his strong feeling that America should create a style of its own and break away from copying the English Georgian houses. This combination of fashion and politics gave birth to the Federal style. Built of both wood and brick, the earliest Federal style houses were found in Colonial cities along the eastern seaboard. The style began to spread in the 1820s and 1830s, thanks in part to builders' handbooks. The Federal style returned to popularity in the twentieth century when Colonial Revivals were in vogue. It can be found in suburban homes of the 1920s and townhouses of the 1970s, and the style is still common in America.

Focus on Features

The rounded arch of ancient Roman architecture was transformed into the *fanlight* of the Federal style. This semicircular window located above the door takes its name from the shape of a fully opened woman's hand fan. The fanlight functions to let light into the entrance hall while maintaining privacy. Handbooks such as *The American Builder's Companion* by Asher Benjamin provided "how-to" instructions for building a fanlight and various classical columns. An *Ionic column* is an elegant Greek column easily distinguished from the other classical columns by its capital, which has volutes that look like upside-down scrolls.

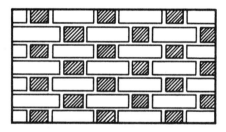

The pattern created by *headers* and *stretchers* determines the *brick bond*. When headers and stretchers alternate in one row it is called *Flemish bond*, a pattern often found in the finest brick buildings.

A *stringcourse* is a projecting belt of brick that divides the house horizontally. The stringcourse may have originally served a structural function to provide reinforcement where the floor joists were cut into the wall.

GREEK REVIVAL

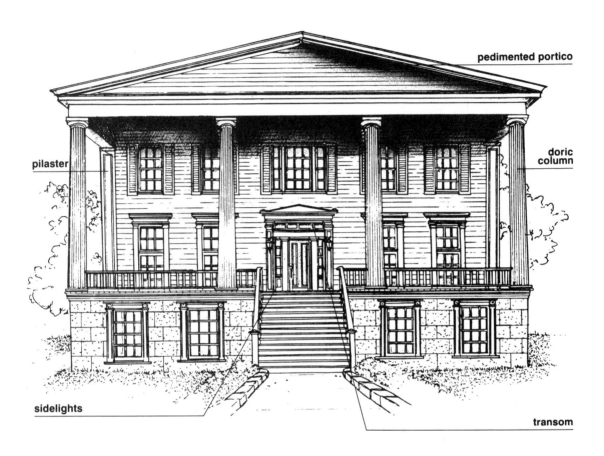

pedimented portico

doric column

pilaster

sidelights

transom

At a Glance: When you conjure up memories of the plantation houses of the Old South, it is likely that you are picturing the Greek Revival style. The portico of classical columns that distinguishes this style is designed to resemble an ancient Greek temple. Typically these houses have a broad central hall with four rooms on each floor and a transom over the front door. They are often painted white to look like marble. Symmetry rules both inside and out; even the formal boxwood gardens in the original Greek Revival homes were perfectly symmetrical.

Background: The heart and soul of the Greek Revival style belong to the South, although examples can be found in New England and elsewhere in America. In the South this style reached the height of its popularity in the years just before the Civil War, a time when Americans romanticized the past, particularly the ancient classical world. The Federal style, based on Roman design elements, was replaced in popularity by this classical style based on earlier Greek elements. You can easily tell the difference between the Federal and Greek Revival styles by looking at the entrance. On a Greek Revival house you will find a transom over the door instead of a fanlight. The Greek Revival style lost popularity in the Victorian era, but reappeared in revised form around the turn of the century when the Neoclassical style became popular.

Focus on Features

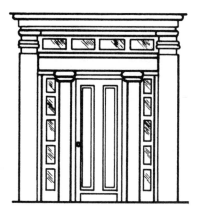

A *transom* is a flat bar of windows atop the door. The transom and *sidelights* are typical features of the Greek Revival style. They represent the lintel-and-post form of Greek construction, whereas the fanlight of the Federal style represents the arched construction of the ancient Romans.

A *Doric column* is one of the plainest of the classical columns. It was developed by the Dorian Greeks and has a simple cushion capital. The vertical ridges are called *flutes* and were thought to represent the draping folds of a gown. The flat column against the wall, echoing the Doric column in front, is called a *pilaster*. *Engaged columns* are not flat but half-round and attached to the wall.

Portico comes from *porticus*, the Latin word for porch, and designates a structure consisting of a roof supported by columns. The *pediment* is the triangular gable end of the roof over the portico. This was a typical feature of Greek temples, of which the Parthenon is the most famous example. This triangle shape is also used as a decorative hood over windows and doors.

NEOCLASSICAL

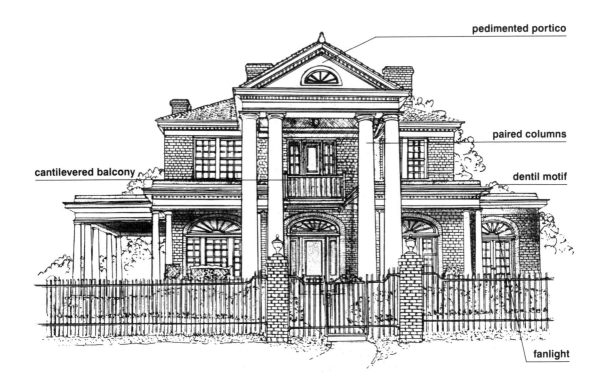

pedimented portico

paired columns

dentil motif

cantilevered balcony

fanlight

At a Glance: The distinguishing feature of a Neoclassical house is a portico of white classical columns. Ionic, Corinthian, or Doric columns, dormer windows, and side porches are elements common to the Neoclassical style of the 1900s to 1940s.

Background: *Neo* means new, and *classical*, at least in architecture, implies the use of white columns. The Neoclassical style was born in the late-nineteenth century when, after decades of ornamental Victorian homes with gingerbread and turrets, Americans began looking fondly back to the classical styles. This fashion spread throughout America thanks in large part to the Columbian Expo, a world's fair held in Chicago in 1893. Along the lagoons of the fairgrounds Americans saw temporary white pavilions adorned with columns, domes, and arches galore. By the turn of the century, almost every town and suburb boasted a Neoclassical house. The style was particularly popular in the 1940s as a result of the movie *Gone with the Wind*. During this period the term *Southern Colonial* was incorrectly attached to the style; homes with classical porticos were popular in the southern states during the antebellum period, not the Colonial era. Neoclassical style houses are still as popular today as they were at the turn of the century. Adding classical columns is an easy way to create a sense of grandeur and add a historical touch to a house.

Focus on Features

A *cantilevered balcony* is one that extends out from the wall without visible means of support. The balcony is supported by beams which run deep into the wall, parallel to the interior floor joists.

Neoclassical homes built around the turn of the century often have paired columns from the Beaux Arts tradition. The École des Beaux Arts in Paris was considered by many to be *the* place to study architecture at the time. The school's approach was to train architects in the study of ancient monuments and to use those classical design principles to create modern buildings.

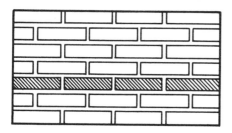

Homes of red brick with white columns are often called *Jeffersonian Classical*, after Thomas Jefferson, who designed his own home, Monticello, along the same lines.

The art of *brick veneer* was mastered around 1900. Brick veneer is a non-load-bearing outside wall of bricks applied onto a frame structure. A brick bond consisting of all stretchers is a clue that the brick is veneer.

COLONIAL REVIVAL

hip roof

sun parlor

clapboard

fanlight

entrance hood

At a Glance: On the outside, Colonial Revival houses display a love of the traditional; on the inside, they have all the modern conveniences, such as central heat, plumbing, and modern kitchens. They typically have clapboard exteriors and windows with at least six panes of glass in each sash. Front windows usually have ornamental shutters which do not open and shut. Instead of a front porch, Colonial Revival houses usually have a side porch known as a sun parlor. These houses often sit on large grassy lawns and wear ornamental shrubbery around their foundations.

Background: The term Colonial Revival is a catchall term to describe houses that were designed to evoke memories of the American Colonial style. Colonial motifs are mixed and matched with more modern design elements. In the history of American home building, copying historic styles is nothing new. The first wave of Colonial Revival rolled into American fashion in 1876, when we celebrated our nation's hundredth anniversary at the Philadelphia Centennial Exposition. The second wave of Colonial Revival hit American neighborhoods from the 1920s through the 1940s, when the World Wars stimulated patriotism. The Bicentennial celebration of 1976 renewed interest once again in Colonial Revival homes.

Focus on Features

A *hip* (or *hipped*) *roof* is one which slopes upward on four sides. The angle at the intersection of two sloping roof surfaces is called a *hip*.

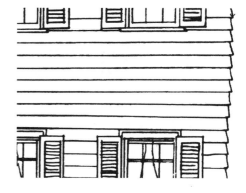

Clapboards (also called *weatherboards* or *lapboards*) are overlapping, horizontal wooden boards. Clapboards are traditionally thicker along the lower edge than the upper edge, a design which facilitates the shedding of water.

An *entrance hood* shelters the door like the hood of an elegant raincoat. From the 1920s to the 1940s these hoods were commonly supported by large brackets with fanciful scrolls.

Around 1920, side porches, or *sun parlors*, became popular and began to replace front porches.

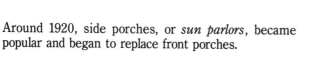

CAPE COD

central chimney

dormer window

clapboard

shutters

six-over-six window

At a Glance: Cape Cod houses are one- or one-and-a-half-story clapboard cottages with no front porch and very little ornament. Windows have small panes of glass and shutters. The gable roof typically has a central chimney and dormer windows. Inside, these houses generally have small rooms, a tiny kitchen and bath, and hardwood floors.

Background: The Cape Cod is a Colonial style that originated in the Massachusetts seaside village of the same name. What started as a quaint Colonial dwelling in a small New England village became one of the most popular house styles in America from the 1920s through the 1950s, and it is still popular today. The modest Cape Cod cottage proved to be a favorite among developers and architects who wanted to provide practical, low-cost housing. The style was particularly common after World War II, when returning veterans used VA loans to finance their first homes. It should be noted that not all Cape Cod houses were built for families of modest income, but even the larger Cape Cods maintain a certain quaintness.

Focus on Features

Dormer comes from the French word *dormir*, meaning to sleep. It follows that dormer windows are found in roofs, since they allow light and ventilation into the attic area, which was traditionally used as the children's "dormitory" or sleeping area. A building is said to have a *half-story* if an area in the roof has living space.

The picturesque *picket fence* is as American as Tom Sawyer. Early fences were designed to keep animals out of the garden; today, however, fences are often designed to keep people out. One of the most prominent landscape features of suburbs at the turn of the twenty-first century is the entrance gate and fence.

Exterior *shutters* originally protected the house from storms and unwelcome visitors. Interior shutters helped the house adapt to the climate; with shutters closed, windows could still be opened to allow ventilation. This function has been taken over by screened windows and venetian blinds. In the twentieth century, most shutters are nailed to the wall and are purely decorative.

GARRISON

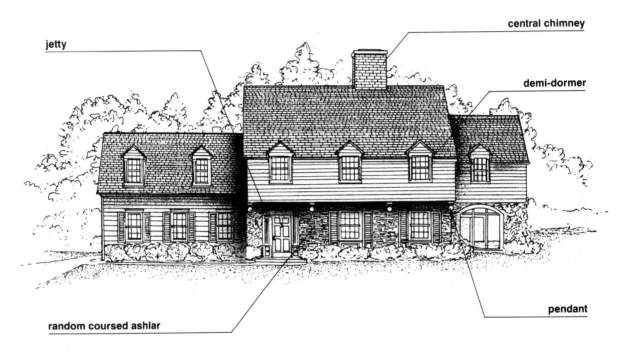

central chimney

jetty

demi-dormer

pendant

random coursed ashlar

At a Glance: The focal point of the Garrison house is the jetty, or overhang, of the second story. The first story of the house is often stone and the overhanging second story of clapboard. Many of these houses have a massive central chimney. The main ornament is the combination of materials and textures under the jetty.

Background: The jetty overhang was a common feature in English medieval construction, as well as in early forts or "garrisons" in America. It is common to find ornamental drops shaped like cannonballs under the jetty, no doubt a reference to its garrison origins. Only a few Colonial Garrison houses with jetties survive, and most of these are found in New England. In the Historical Revival fashions from 1920 on, Garrison houses (also called New England Colonial) became popular in suburbs across America.

Focus on Features

Foundation plantings are shrubs planted at the base of the house. This landscape feature became popular around 1900 when homes were constructed with *continuous foundations* and basements containing plumbing and central heating facilities. Especially in warm climates, earlier houses often had *pier foundations*.

The *jetty*, a typical feature of medieval buildings, is a second story which juts out slightly over the first story. In America, jetties were associated with fortresses, hence the name *garrison*. The decorative pendants hanging down look like cannonballs, reinforcing the visual image of a fort.

Often the first story is made of rough, squared building stones called *ashlar*. When laid in horizontal rows, this is called *coursed ashlar*.

DUTCH

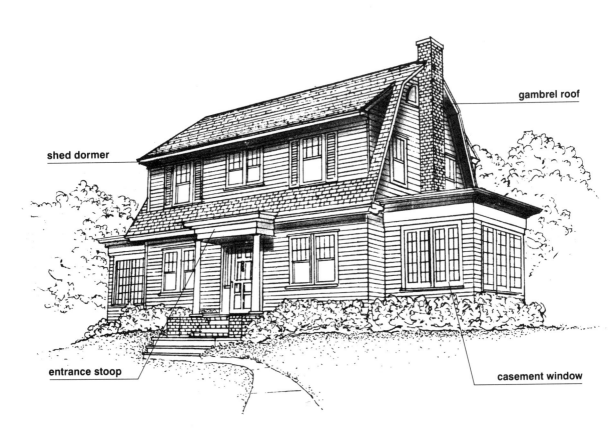

gambrel roof

shed dormer

casement window

entrance stoop

At a Glance: The main feature of the Dutch (or Dutch Colonial) style is the distinctive gambrel roof, with two pitches on each side. This roofline, typically associated with barns, provides the maximum amount of living space within the roof.

Background: The gambrel roof was commonly found on the barns and homes of early colonists. This distinctive style enjoyed a revival from the 1920s through the 1950s and was one of the most popular styles offered for sale in the Sears, Roebuck catalog. Sears was in the business of mail-order houses from about 1908 to 1940. In 1921 they advertised a Dutch Colonial house called the "Martha Washington," which had seven rooms and one bath and sold for $2,688. For that price, Sears sent you everything needed to construct the house on your lot, including the doors, stairs, windows, walls, floors, plumbing, and light fixtures. In its 1939 catalog, Sears boasted that more than 100,000 families were living in their "ordered by mail, sent by rail" homes. Although Sears was the largest, it was by no means the only mail-order house company.

Focus on Features

Dutch style houses typically have *shed dormers*. Instead of having a gable roof, the dormer has a roof with a long slope facing the road. These wide dormers often contain several small windows and have the advantage of adding more head room to the attic area. It is not uncommon to have a screened sleeping porch in the shed dormer.

An *entrance stoop* is a covered platform, one bay wide. In architecture the width of a building is measured in *bays*, defined by regularly repeated elements such as windows or doors. An entrance stoop provides just enough roof to stand under and be sheltered from the elements. Unlike a front porch, a stoop does not offer space for chairs.

The side sun parlor has *casement windows*. Unlike *sash windows*, which slide up or down within a frame, casement windows are hinged and swing out.

SALTBOX

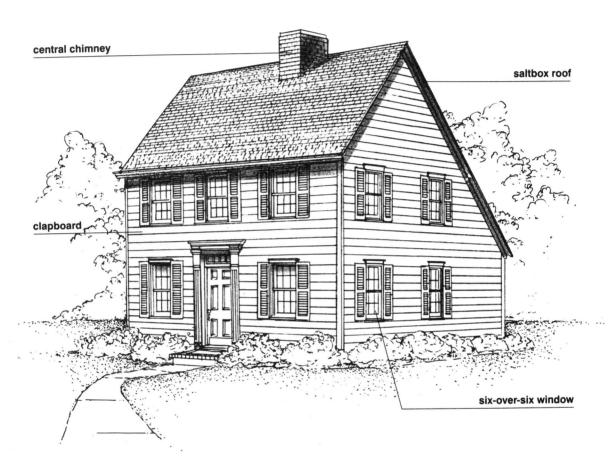

central chimney

saltbox roof

clapboard

six-over-six window

At a Glance: The distinctive silhouette of the roof, with a short pitch in front and a long low slope to the rear, is the major characteristic of the Saltbox style. In the South, the long rear slope of the roof is called a *catslide*. The Saltbox is typically a two-story clapboard house with minimal ornamentation. The central chimney is a typical feature of this style.

Background: The shape of the roof is similar to an early Colonial salt container, hence the name. This style originated in the Colonial era in and around New England; it spread across America through mail-order plans and was particularly popular from 1920 to the 1970s.

20

Focus on Features

The massive *central chimney* is a typical feature of most New England Colonial houses, including the Saltbox. In the South it was more common to find chimneys at the exterior ends of the house. The size of the chimney indicates that the fireplace was used for burning large logs. Coal-burning fireplaces, common in the Victorian era, were slender and tall. The central fireplace was suitable to the cold climate because heat radiated from the center of the house.

Six-panel doors are a typical Colonial fixture. Some call this a *cross-and-open-Bible door*; the cross is formed by the upper panels, the Bible by the lower. *Christian door* is another name for this familiar design. The six-panel door is surrounded by fluted Doric pilasters on each side and a transom above.

The trim around the window is called the *window surround*. The *lintel*, or molding above the window, acts to shelter the window from rain or snow.

CREOLE (COASTAL) COTTAGE

dormer window

gallery

pier foundation

lattice

At A Glance: The distinctive Creole, or Coastal, cottage features a high hip roof punctuated with dormer windows. This roof creates an umbrella effect over its deep porches, or galleries. Tall windows and French doors lead from each room directly out onto the galleries, which also serve as exterior hallways. Original Creole houses are elevated above the ground on pier foundations of brick or stone.

Background: The French colonists settling around the Mississippi River created a house form particularly well suited to the hot, humid climate of Louisiana and Mississippi. The high hip or gable roofs allow hot air to rise, leaving the rooms below cooler. Pier foundations allow breezes to circulate underneath, cooling the house and at the same time preventing rot and termite infestation. In the 1980s, the raised Creole Cottage style began to make its way into suburbs of southern cities, coastal communities, and lake developments.

Focus on Features

Pier foundations are a boon in hot or humid climates, since they cool houses and protect them from rot at the same time. *Lattice*, thin strips of wood in a criss-cross pattern, added ornament between the piers and kept unwanted animals from beneath the house. Indoor plumbing and central heat made it necessary to underpin pier foundations, making a continuous foundation.

No country has a stronger attachment to the *front porch* than America. The porch itself goes by several names. A classical porch is a *portico*. A Victorian porch is a *verandah*. In Charleston long side porches are called *piazzas*, and in Louisiana they are called *galleries*. Porches are often the most ornamental part of a house. They serve as outdoor living rooms, as sheltered entrances to the house, as places for outdoor meals, and sometimes as second-story sleeping quarters. The well was often located on the rear porch. In the South, one end of a porch was sometimes enclosed to create a place where traveling preachers and teachers could spend a night. These travelers' rooms were architectural proof of southern hospitality. Eventually the front porch lost favor to the side porch and then to the rear patio. Recently the front porch has been restored to its rightful place as an important part of the American home.

NOTES

NOTES

VICTORIAN

QUEEN ANNE

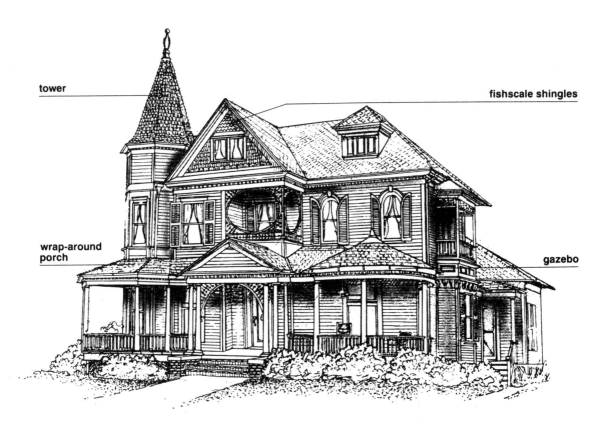

tower

fishscale shingles

wrap-around porch

gazebo

At a Glance: Queen Anne style houses fit into the ornamental Victorian category, typically incorporating a tower, a wrap-around porch, and an asymmetrical roofline of gables and hips. Windows are of every shape and size. The exterior texture is varied, often including fishscale shingles in the gable, gingerbread, and spindles around the porch. Towers, bays, and cut-aways create a playful arrangement of exterior shapes, made possible by balloon-frame construction.

Background: The term Queen Anne was coined by a nineteenth-century English architect named Richard Norman Shaw (despite the fact that the style has little to do with the Renaissance architectural fashions that were popular during the rule of Queen Anne (1702-14)). Queen Anne houses sprang up like mushrooms in small towns and cities across America from 1880 to 1900. The style was popularized through periodicals, as well as through the mail-order house plans of George Barber, an entrepreneurial Victorian architect from Knoxville, Tennessee. Barber's designs were published in 1891 in his plan book *Cottage Souvenir*. Complete architectural plans sold for as little as fifteen to twenty-five dollars, and Barber later began shipping pre-cut homes by rail to cities throughout the country.

Focus on Features

Victorians were particularly fond of bringing nature into the house. One way to do this was to attach a *gazebo*, formerly a landscape feature, to the corner of the verandah. These open-sided, conical-roofed structures were created to provide a sheltered place to sit and enjoy the scenic view.

Queen Anne houses are characterized by *towers* or *turrets*. The difference between a tower and a turret is that a tower starts at the base of a house, while a turret juts out from the wall or roof. Sometimes stairs are placed in the towers, but more often they serve no special function inside the house other than to create an interesting corner in a room.

The playful arrangement of exterior shapes was made possible by *balloon-frame construction*. A lightweight framework of standard machine-milled two-by-fours, held together by machine-made nails, replaced the heavy timbers used in post-and-beam construction. First used in Chicago, balloon-frame construction freed Victorian builders from the square design. A similar construction technique, called *platform-frame*, is used to construct homes today.

CARPENTER GOTHIC

bargeboard

gingerbread

bonnet porch

At a Glance: The vertical emphasis of this Victorian Gothic style is created by steeply pitched front gables, ranging in number from one to three. The jigsaw was used to create ornaments for the Carpenter Gothic style: bargeboards for the gables and gingerbread woodwork for the verandahs, which looked vaguely like the stone tracery in medieval churches.

Background: The Gothic novels of Sir Walter Scott helped set the mood for the mid-nineteenth-century battle over America's latest Romantic style. The medieval emerged victorious over the classical, resulting in Gothic elements being added to myriad houses. The Gothic style was first applied to American homes by architect A. J. Davis, but it was his friend A. J. Downing who popularized the style. Downing promoted the Gothic, or "pointed," style in his 1850 book, *The Architecture of Country Houses*. He described the style as picturesque and went on to recommend that it be painted in muted natural colors such as buff, grey, tan, and fawn to ensure that the house would harmonize with its surroundings. The Carpenter Gothic style enjoyed widespread popularity from 1850 to the 1880s, especially in small towns and rural areas.

Focus on Features

The *bargeboard*, also called the *vergeboard*, is the decorative board covering the end of the gable. Bargeboards are an ornamental element of many Victorian homes. This bargeboard is designed to look like a medieval roof truss with a central king post and braces to each side. Bargeboards represented to the Victorians an irresistible opportunity to ornament the house. Designs include birds, hearts, vines, and geometric shapes, among others. Local woodworkers could create bargeboards which individualized homes, even going so far as to incorporate the owner's initials and date of construction into a design. Ready-made bargeboards could be ordered from mills and shipped by rail anywhere in the country. The Gordon-Van Tine Company from Davenport, Iowa, advertised an adjustable bargeboard in their 1915 catalog, ranging in price from seventy-five cents to $1.70.

One-story shed porches with a hip at each end of the roof are sometimes called *bonnet porches*. Victorian porches are typically accented with *gingerbread woodwork* — i.e., flat wood cut into fanciful shapes with a jigsaw. Gingerbread woodwork gives a house the appearance of an old-fashioned paper valentine. The term *gingerbread* most likely was borrowed from gingerbread houses, which dripped with ornament.

SECOND EMPIRE

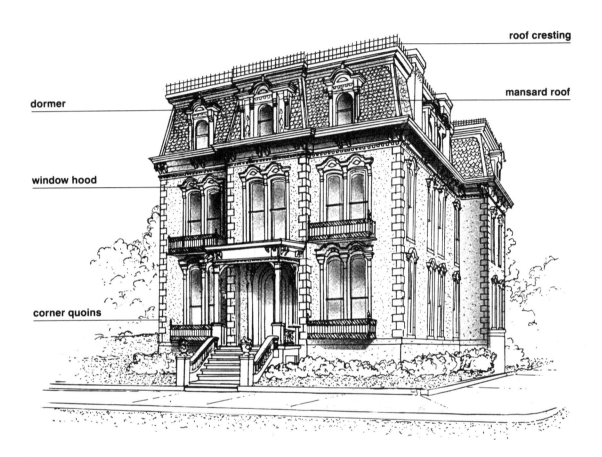

roof cresting

mansard roof

dormer

window hood

corner quoins

At a Glance: The most recognizable feature of the Second Empire style is the mansard roof. The mansard roof actually has two slopes: a low-pitched, almost flat slope on top and a steeply pitched, almost vertical slope below. This boxy shape combined with dormer windows allowed a full upper story in the attic space.

Background: The mansard roof was the height of fashion during the Second Empire period in mid-nineteenth-century France. The Louvre in Paris is perhaps the most famous example of the style. As it spread to American shores, Second Empire became a favorite style for public buildings during the Grant administration. It remained a popular Victorian house style for middle-class rowhouses and the mansions of the wealthy from about 1860 through 1890. In the mid-1960s, builders rediscovered the advantages of the mansard roof, and extra space was created in apartment buildings and even ranch houses. This new mansard style was popular from about 1960 to 1980, when rustic wood shingles were used for the roof.

Focus on Features

The *mansard roof*, named for seventeenth-century French architect Francois Mansard, may have developed as a clever way of avoiding extra taxes. According to this theory, buildings in Paris were taxed according to their height—i.e., how many stories they had. The steep pitch of the mansard roof provided enough space for additional rooms, but since it was technically in the roof, it wasn't taxed as another story.

Slate is a common material for mansard roofs, both in France and here in America.

Highly ornamental dormer windows are almost always featured on mansard roofs, and *metal roof crestings* often outline the very top. In America, Second Empire came to be associated with haunted houses, an association surely promoted by Hollywood's tendency to use the style in horror movies such as "Psycho."

ITALIANATE

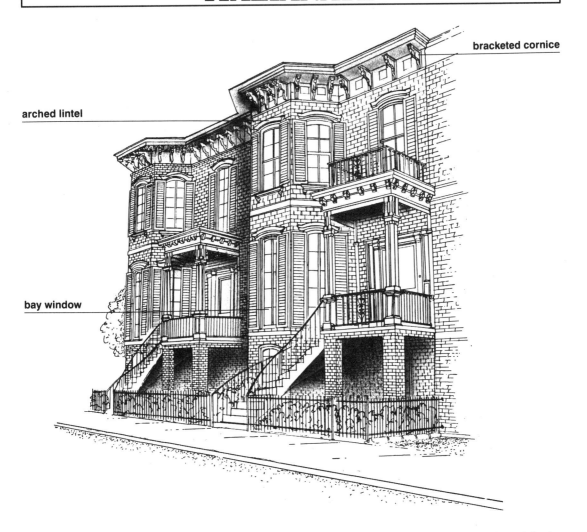

bracketed cornice

arched lintel

bay window

At a Glance: Italianate houses have been described as rectangular buildings with brackets dripping from their wide eaves. Also typical of the style are arched and bay windows, with lintels or window hoods.

Background: The style is derived from the urban mansions of Italian merchant princes and the rambling bracketed designs of rural Italian farmhouses. The Italianate style became popular in America as early as 1840 through the books of A. J. Downing, who promoted the use of this bracketed style with a tower for suburban villas. From the 1870s through the 1890s, this style was adopted for urban townhouses. Brownstones in New York and brick rowhouses in Baltimore often displayed eave brackets, window hoods, and dormer windows. The fact that cast iron hoods and iron railings could be shipped from foundries to any city by train helped to promote Italianate ornamentation.

Focus on Features

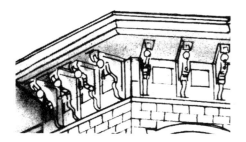

Large *brackets* supporting wide eaves are so closely associated with the Italianate style that it is also referred to as the Bracketed style. A bracket is designed to serve a structural purpose; it projects from a wall to support the weight of something other than the wall, such as the roof. But brackets can also be extremely decorative, with incised patterns, scrolls, and drops or pendants hanging from the top. Brackets are commonly grouped in pairs.

Urban townhouses often employ *bay projections* with windows on three sides as a means to increase the amount of light entering the house.

When a full basement is located below a raised entrance to a house, it is referred to as an *English basement*. The kitchen and service areas are located on the bottom level, and steps lead up to the house's front door. The entrance stoop is also likely to have Italianate brackets.

EASTLAKE

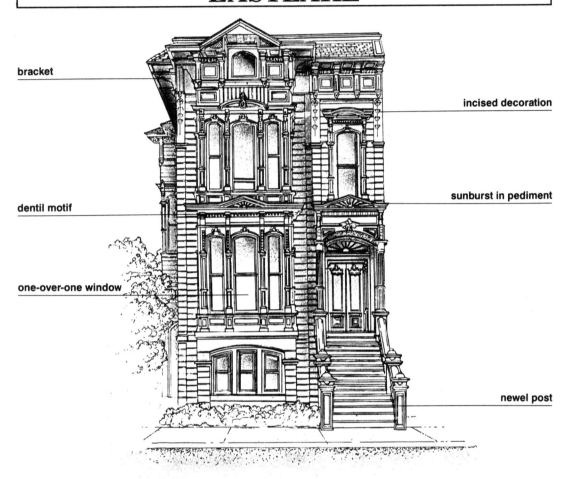

bracket

incised decoration

dentil motif

sunburst in pediment

one-over-one window

newel post

At a Glance: Eastlake was not a style proper, but rather a Victorian recipe for decorative ornament based on popular furniture designs. These eclectic houses borrowed elements from several different styles; Italianate brackets, Gothic gables, and classical columns were all mixed to the visual delight of Victorian homeowners. The style is named for Charles Eastlake, an English furniture designer and author of the popular Victorian guide to interior design *Hints on Household Taste*.

Background: Around 1890, it seemed that anything and everything was a source of inspiration for exterior ornament, including popular books, steamboats, industrial machines, flowers, plants, birds, and furniture design. Especially in San Francisco, Charles Eastlake's ideas for furniture were enthusiastically adopted for architectural ornament. For example, designs intended for table legs were used for porch columns. When Eastlake himself learned of the American "Eastlake" style, he announced that he regretted that his name was associated with "a phase of taste in architecture...with which I can have no real sympathy, and which by all accounts seems to be extravagant and bizarre." The turn of the twenty-first century is once again seeing the emergence of a fashion for ornamental, eclectic homes.

Focus on Features

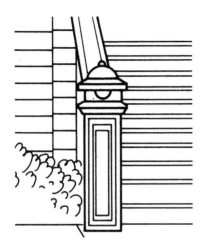

The ornamental post at the base of the stairs, the *newel post*, is an important design feature of many Victorian houses. Some newel posts serve as a base for sculpture or light fixtures; others hold what was referred to as a *mortgage button*. When the mortgage on the house was paid off, an ivory button was proudly set into the newel post.

A pediment displaying a sunburst design is another popular Victorian motif. Some say it reflects the idea that the industrial revolution was the dawn of a new era. Others say that the design alludes to the slogan popular during the rule of Queen Victoria, that the sun never sets on the British Empire.

Incised ornaments were thin lines cut out of the surface of the wood. Incised ornaments, along with blocky, knob-like designs, were typical features of Eastlake furniture.

ROMANESQUE

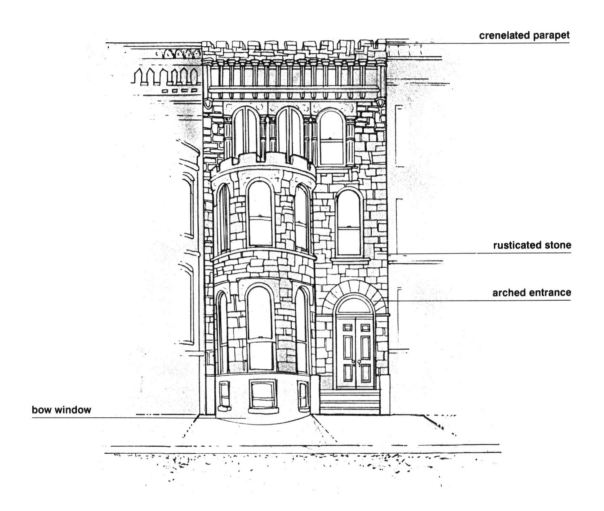

crenelated parapet

rusticated stone

arched entrance

bow window

At a Glance: Romanesque houses are massive masonry structures of rough-cut stones, towers, and rounded arches. Roofs are outlined with crenelated parapets, and arches are supported by squat columns.

Background: In the Victorian era, a wealthy man's home could truly be his castle, though it was likely to be modeled after medieval Romanesque fortresses or churches. In America, the Romanesque style had its origins in Chicago and is so closely attached to the work of architect Henry Hobson Richardson that it is often called Richardson Romanesque. The style was limited to architect-designed homes of the wealthy and urban rowhouses from around 1880 to the early 1900s.

Focus on Features

The *crenelated parapet* of the roof gives a Romanesque home the look of a castle. A *parapet* is part of the wall which rises above the roof. A *crenelated* parapet is topped with blocks in a pattern of repeated indentations. From movies we know that soldiers shot at invaders from the crenelated parapet of the embattled castle or fortress.

A *bow window* is a type of bay window. It has a semi-circular shape like a drawn bow ready to shoot an arrow.

The walls of this home are made of *rusticated stone —* i.e., stone that has been tooled to give it a rough, natural texture. At one time, granite was commonly rusticated and used as a building material. However, by the turn of the twentieth century, cast stone — concrete poured into molds with a rusticated pattern — was more often used for this purpose.

STEAMBOAT GOTHIC

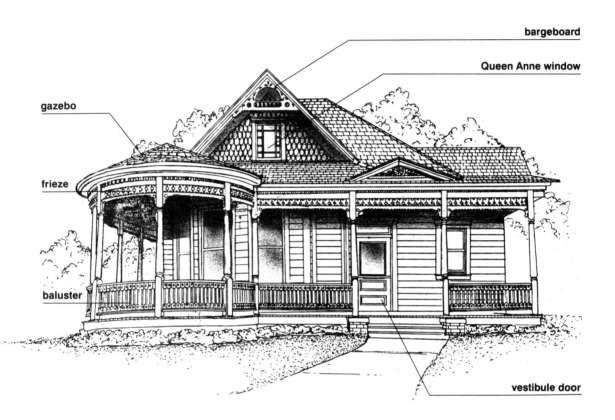

bargeboard

Queen Anne window

gazebo

frieze

baluster

vestibule door

At a Glance: The main feature of the Steamboat style is the porch, which has decorative railing at the bottom (balusters) and at the top (frieze). The bargeboard often has a captain's wheel, and wave designs are commonly depicted in the woodwork.

Background: This porch style transformed a Victorian home into a romanticized image of the Mississippi steamboats described by Mark Twain in his popular novels. Steamboat decoration was popular first in the southern states, then spread westward from the 1880s to 1900. Railroads crisscrossed the nation, making it possible to deliver architectural features such as balusters or bargeboards from a mill in Iowa to a house in Kentucky in a matter of days. In the late 1970s, homes with Steamboat porches once again appeared in suburbs.

Focus on Features

Anatomy of a Victorian porch: Support is supplied by *turned columns*, solid pieces of wood turned on a lathe machine, which shapes blocks of wood into circular forms. *Column brackets* arc from the column to support the frieze above. The *frieze* consists of the decorative spindle railing and dentil motif at the top of the porch, just below the cornice. The *cornice* is the molded projection above the frieze and under the roof eave. The *balustrade* consists of the railings and handrail connecting the lower part of the columns.

The distinctive *vestibule door* was a popular front door in the Victorian era. It has a single large pane of glass set into its top half and one or more wood panels below.

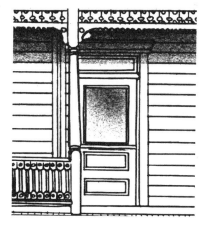

SHINGLE

shingles

ribbon window

wrap-around porch

At a Glance: The Shingle style is easy to identify since the whole exterior wall surface is covered with wood shingles. These asymmetrical homes often have steeply pitched roofs, expansive porches, and windows grouped in ribbons.

Background: These houses were originally built along the northeast seaside as millionaires' cottages, flourishing from 1880 into the 1910s. Most Shingle style houses were architect-designed, and the style was never widely popular in mass-produced homes. In the 1970s, architects revived shingle-clad homes for seaside and resort communities.

Focus on Features

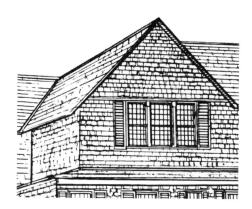

Even before the appearance of the Shingle style, *wood shingles* had long been used as a sheathing for American homes, especially in coastal areas of the Northeast. Originally, shingles had to be split by hand, but in the Victorian era steam-powered wood-working machines made it possible to create decorative woodwork and building materials in a fraction of the time it would have taken by hand. One such machine, the shingle maker, was introduced at the Philadelphia Centennial Exposition of 1876, and from that time shingles could be produced quickly and economically. Shingles were commonly used to ornament gables, but in the Shingle style, walls were also covered in this decorative manner. Shingles were usually stained and not painted.

A *wrap-around porch* encircles two or more sides of a house.

Vines were a popular Victorian landscape treatment. They climbed up columns, porches, and walls, blurring the distinction between the house and its natural surroundings.

NOTES

NOTES

EUROPEAN

REGENCY

At a Glance: Regency homes have a smooth stucco exterior with symmetrically arranged windows and classical details. Arches, columns, and corner quoins are common. Palladian windows are particularly popular in late-twentieth-century versions of the style. In many ways, the Regency style looks like a red brick Georgian house which has been given a coat of stucco. Like the Palladian Georgian style, Regency homes often have a projecting entrance pavilion.

Background: The Regency style is named for the Prince Regent, later George IV, who ruled the British Empire from 1811 to 1830. Early American examples of this elegant, showy style date from the 1820s and are rare indeed, but from 1920 to 1940 the Regency style became a favorite of Historical Revival architects. Regency style houses enjoyed widespread popularity again in the 1980s and 1990s, when builders and architects created ornamental suburban homes with corner quoins and Palladian windows.

Focus on Features

Stucco is a type of exterior plaster traditionally used as a protective coating for soft brick. Early stucco was made of lime and sand mixed with water; later, portland cement was added as a binder.

Quoins (pronounced "coins") are the blocks found at the corners of a building. In early masonry construction, the quoins were massive stones which provided structural reinforcement; later they became purely decorative.

The *pavilion* is the part of the building which projects out from the wall surface. A central projecting pavilion is a common feature of late Georgian and Regency architecture.

Facade is the French word for face. In architecture, the term usually denotes the front face of a building.

BAROQUE

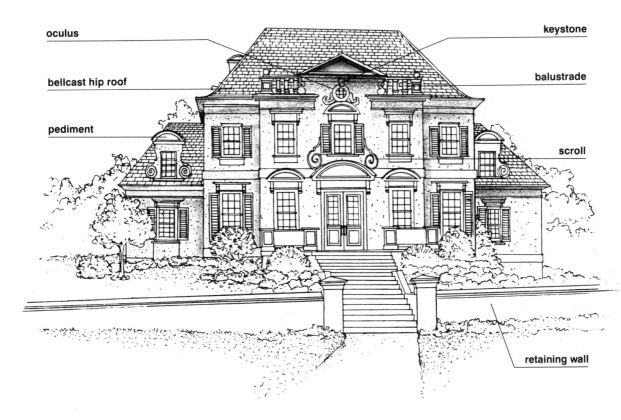

oculus

keystone

bellcast hip roof

balustrade

pediment

scroll

retaining wall

At a Glance: Baroque homes employ classical ornament on a monumental scale. Windows and doors are topped with keystones or pediments. Balustrades add elegance to roof lines, balconies, and patios. Smooth stucco facades are sculptured into ornamental compositions by corner quoins, arches, and panels. A typical feature of the Baroque style is vertical composition, created by linking the doorway with windows above by scrolls and pediments.

Background: The word *baroque* was first used to describe a pearl of irregular shape. The term was subsequently applied to the architecture of the late Renaissance period in Italy, a time when architects unleashed their creative expression with great exuberance. In America, Baroque homes were designed by architects who had traveled to Europe to study ancient buildings. The suburban villas of wealthy Americans began to display Baroque embellishments in the early years of the twentieth century, and extremely ornamental Baroque houses have again become popular among builders as the century comes to a close.

Focus on Features

A *bellcast hip roof* is one which is flared at the eaves.

Windows on a home are like the eyes of a person's face. They admit light, provide visions of the world outside, and can be made up to be quite decorative. Plato said the eyes are the pathway to the soul. Similarly, the windows of a home—their size, placement, shape, and ornamentation—reveal much about its style and even provide a clue to the date of construction. The uppermost circular window is called an *oculus* (from the Latin word for eye). The windows of this Baroque home have decorative *surrounds*.

The "S" form of the *scroll* on console or bracket shapes is a common feature of Baroque design. "Why have a straight line when you could have a curved line?" was the sentiment of this style. The spiral scroll is called a *volute*.

A *retaining wall* functions to keep topsoil from sliding down a slope. Often made of stone, brick, concrete, or stucco, it defines the front yard by separating it from the public space of the sidewalk.

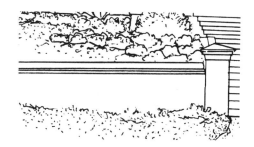

CHATEAUESQUE

Roman arch

demi-dormer

keystone

hip roof

French shutters

At a Glance: The most prominent feature of this elegant French style is the steeply pitched hip roof, which is often made of slate. Arched windows and dormers, French doors, quoins, and stucco or stone walls combine to add to the rambling appearance of a French chateau (i.e., castle or country estate). These grand houses typically have an entrance foyer featuring a magnificent stairway, and some have towers or turrets.

Background: This architectural fantasy was popular among the very wealthy at the turn of the twentieth century and is again enjoying popularity in the century's closing decades. The best known example of the Chateauesque style is probably the Biltmore House in Asheville, North Carolina, built by the Vanderbilt family in the late-nineteeth century. Today's versions of this style feature multi-car garages instead of the traditional stables.

Focus on Features

Formal, elegant arched entrances and entrance towers or turrets are popular.

A *dormer* is a window in the roof. A *demi-dormer* (from the French word for half) starts in the wall and extends partially into the roof. Windows of this type are also known as *wall dormers*.

The distinguishing features of a French chateau are the arched dormers and the high-pitched hip roof, often made of *slate*. Slate is a type of stone which cleaves easily into flat sheets. Because of its weight, slate is particularly suited for steep-pitched roofs and is commonly found on French mansard and hip roofs. Slate is often a gray-blue color, but also comes in reddish and green tones. When cared for properly, a slate roof can last for centuries. Today, synthetic slate materials are also available for roofing.

RENAISSANCE

wide eaves

pergola

engaged column

Palladian window

At a Glance: The Renaissance style house is formal and elegant. It has a wide hip roof, with eaves extending to shelter the walls. Windows and doors are arched. The entrance is often flanked by classical columns.

Background: Renaissance merchants and bankers in Italy built symmetrical homes with a classical grandeur that expressed their education, good taste, and wealth. American architects began to use similar designs at the turn of the twentieth century. Italian Renaissance style villas were typically architect-designed mansions...typically, but not always. The villa illustrated here is identical to one advertised in the 1918 catalog for Aladdin Homes, a mail-order homes supplier from Bay City, Michigan. This home originally sold for $5,880. Here's how it was described in the catalog: "Like the beautiful everywhere, this house challenges the lover of the artistic and furnishes a concrete example of the stateliness and strength which at the same time is an embodiment of the finest culture." In short, buy this house and you buy culture, taste, and refinement. Aladdin also had a famous "Dollar-A-Knot" Guarantee: the quality of the ready-cut wood was such that they guaranteed to give customers one dollar for every knot they found in the red cedar siding.

Focus on Features

Featured here is the classical three-part *Palladian window*, with its central arched portion flanked by sidelights. Palladio (see Palladian Georgian, p. 4) believed that beauty lay in a combination of historical correctness and perfect proportion.

A *pergola* is an open-air porch or walkway of open framed wood. The roof is supported by regularly spaced columns or posts. Typically, pergolas are garden structures draped with climbing roses or vines. The side porches of this house have pergola designs.

The wide eaves of the low hip roof spread out to protect the plaster walls from direct contact with water. The *eave* is the lower edge of a sloping roof which projects beyond the wall. Roofs without wide eaves rely on gutters to channel water away from the wall of the house.

Other classical touches on this Renaissance villa include the engaged columns and the Roman arches over windows and doors.

MEDITERRANEAN REVIVAL

barrel tile roof

porte-cochere

arcade

baroque column

wrought iron balcony

stucco

At a Glance: The Mediterranean Revival style is marked by an elegant informality, complemented by its barrel tile roof, pastel stucco walls, wrought iron balcony, and arched windows.

Background: The twentieth-century Mediterranean Revival style has its roots in Florida and California, where Spanish colonists built stucco houses with tile roofs and arched openings. This style enjoyed its heyday from the 1920s through the 1940s. In this golden age of Hollywood, movie stars and film producers lived in grand Mediterranean style mansions, which sparked the spread of the style throughout the country. During this same period, the wealthy in Florida also built lavish Mediterranean style houses; visiting tourists often returned home to build houses in this "Palm Beach" manner.

Focus on Features

Tile is one of the oldest roofing materials on record. The thatch of medieval homes proved to be a fire hazard and was outlawed in many urban areas, so square ceramic tile took its place. In the Mediterranean region, it became traditional to mold the clay over a barrel, giving the tile its characteristic semicircular shape. Most *barrel roof tiles* are red, but green was a fairly common color in the past, especially in the 1920s. Tile roofs have a long life span, but, because of their weight, require tremendous roof support. Consequently, interiors of Mediterranean houses often have massive beamed ceilings.

Wrought iron railing, balconies, and light fixtures are a typical decorative feature of the Mediterranean style. Wrought iron is iron which has been forged or twisted into shape by hand, whereas cast iron is iron which has been poured in a molten state into a form or mold. When the hot metal cools, it assumes the shape of the mold.

An *arcade* is a series of two or more arched openings. Baroque *spiral columns* look like twisted candy canes.

SPANISH

hip

curved parapet roof

front patio

At a Glance: The Spanish house typically has stucco walls and a curved parapet roof. It is said that this style introduced the patio, which became an important architectural feature of the American home. This style was commonly used for apartment buildings from the 1920s through the 1940s.

Background: The ancient Spanish Catholic mission churches of California, with their stucco buildings and Baroque details, inspired a house style that came to be known as Spanish Mission. The Pueblo was another Spanish style popular in the West, characterized by flat roofs and walls of adobe or mud brick. This style reached the height of its nationwide popularity from about 1920 to 1940, although the Spanish and Mediterranean styles have long been a favorite in California.

Mediterranean and Spanish style houses are first cousins, and the two terms are often used interchangeably. The main difference is that Mediterranean homes are usually larger and more ornamental.

Focus on Features

The central arch adorning this *parapet* gives it its distinctive Spanish flavor. The opening in the parapet — the *vent* — allows the flow of air in and out of the roof.

Windows with six panes over six panes became a standard builders' stock item between 1920 and 1940. During this same period it became common practice to pair these windows, allowing more light to enter the rooms.

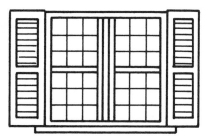

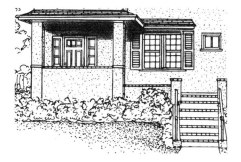

This house has a combination front patio and porch. A *patio* is defined as a paved outdoor space adjacent to a house and often enclosed by walls. The Spanish style is credited with introducing the patio into American home design, and by the 1950s the backyard patio had become a standard feature. By the 1970s the rear deck had replaced the patio in popularity.

ENGLISH COTTAGE

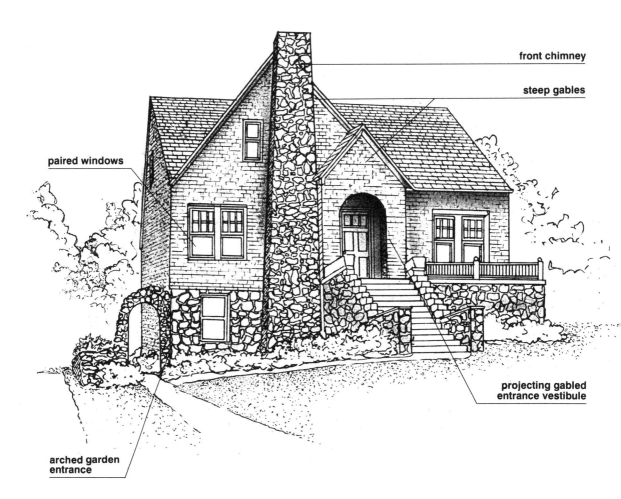

front chimney

steep gables

paired windows

projecting gabled
entrance vestibule

arched garden
entrance

At a Glance: The English Cottage style uses steep gables, grouped windows, a prominent chimney, and a combination of materials to evoke an image of quaint rural England. The Americanized version typically has an entrance vestibule which extends out to welcome the visitor. The majority have brick veneer, often employing a type of textured brick called *tapestry brick*. Inside, wide arched openings create a vista between small rooms.

Background: These homes are often called Cotswold cottages, a reference to the Cotswold Hills of southwest England. Similar cottages of French origin (often including a tower) are referred to as Normandy Cottages. This was one of the most popular house styles in America from 1920 through the 1940s.

Focus on Features

The entrance of an English Cottage house typically consists of a projecting *gabled entrance vestibule* with an arched opening. The irregular massing of steeply pitched gables gives the English Cottage its identity. Overlapping gables are typical features of the style. The stone-arch garden entrance is the ultimate in quaint English design.

The massive chimney is a symbol of technological advance in the history of home building. Prior to development of the chimney, smoke would fill the room of medieval homes and drift out through a hole in the ceiling. With the advent of chimneys, it became possible to have a second floor in houses and to divide interior space. English Cottage houses often have front chimneys.

TUDOR

oriel window

half-timbering

porte-cochere

bay window

At a Glance: The key feature of the Tudor style is the half-timbering in the gables, which is a combination of wood strips and stucco. Tudor houses often have double front gables outlined with bargeboards. Lower stories are typically brick with windows and doors trimmed in stone. Ribbons of small-paned windows, bays, and oriels are common.

Background: The half-timbering in this style is designed to look like a distinctive construction technique that came to characterize the Tudor period (1485-1603). This "Olde English" style has been enduringly popular, but particularly in the late 1920s when it was referred to as "Stockbroker Tudor." The style has also enjoyed a revival since the 1970s.

Focus on Features

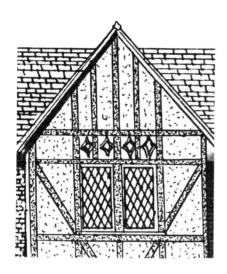

The gables and walls of Tudor houses have decorative half-timbering; i.e., thin strips of wood nailed onto a stucco surface. This sham half-timbering seeks to reproduce in appearance the sixteenth- and seventeenth-century mode of construction wherein the frame of the house consisted of massive beams half the size of tree trunks, corner braces, and roof trusses joined with pegs. The open areas between the timber were filled with brick or woven twigs and covered with a thick coat of plaster. The name half-timber may refer to walls that are half wood and half stucco, or it may refer to the size of the timber, which was half of a cut tree.

The English medieval *oriel window* is a bay window projecting from the upper story of a building.

Porte-cochere is French for coach-door, and the porte-cochere originally acted as a carriage entrance. The horse-drawn carriage would drive into the sheltered opening where passengers would step out and enter the house. In urban areas, the porte-cochere was a carriage entrance leading into a courtyard. In the automobile era, the porte-cochere was a doorway large enough for a car to pass through en route from the street to the car garage, a separate building behind the house. The porte-cochere has evolved into the carport, which is attached to the house in the Ranch style.

JACOBEAN

gabled parapet

dripstone lintels

bay window

At a Glance: The Jacobean is yet another style based on medieval English houses. As with the Tudor, front gables are key features; however, Jacobean houses have masonry walls of brick or stone instead of half-timbering. This style has parapet roofs with tall chimney stacks. Bands of windows punctuate the walls, trimmed in stone and including dripstone lintels. Bay windows are also typical. Entrances are arched and doors often ornamented with tabernacle frames. Brick is common for the walls, while stone is often used for the trim around windows and doors.

Background: The term Jacobean applies to the late-Gothic architectural style popular in England during the rule of James I in the seventeenth century. The style was introduced to America around the turn of the twentieth century and gained popularity in the 1910s and 1920s. The Jacobean style was particularly favored for college and university buildings, but it found its way into the suburbs as well, where it was popular among the upper-middle class from about 1900 to the 1930s.

Focus on Features

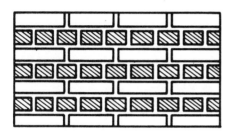

Walls of a Jacobean house are *masonry*: all stone, or, commonly, brick trimmed in stone. These brick walls are laid in *English bond*: one row of headers (the head is the small end of the brick), then one row of strechers (the stretcher is the long side of the brick). Alternate rows of headers and stretchers create a load-bearing brick wall. Builders often create brick veneer walls to look like the more costly English bond by using headers which are cut short. Windows, doors, and roof coping are often trimmed in a light-colored stone, or perhaps a concrete substitute.

Windows take up a large portion of wall space in Jacobean houses. *Bay windows* (often having three sides with glass) are prized because they introduce a great deal of light into the room. It is also common to find one window stacked on top of another to create a vertical shaft of light.

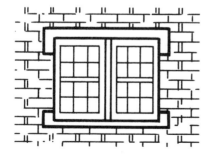

Dripstone lintels around the doors and windows are a common medieval feature.

MEDIEVAL MANOR

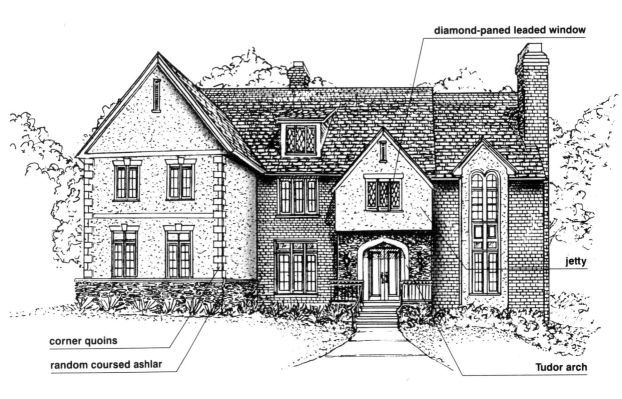

diamond-paned leaded window

jetty

corner quoins

random coursed ashlar

Tudor arch

At a Glance: Medieval motifs such as the jetty overhang, the diamond-shaped casement windows, and the massive chimney all combine to make a modern house appear centuries old. The rambling form of the house is carefully designed to give the appearance of having been added to over the years. This style uses a combination of materials such as stone, brick, and stucco.

Background: In western medieval Europe, the mansion of a lord and the lands over which he ruled comprised his manor. The Medieval Manor style, particularly popular in the 1980s and early 1990s, is yet another way to satisfy the American hunger for the ancient, for the look of age and stability in a world of change.

Focus on Features

Employing a combination of materials is one sure way to make a building look as though it has grown over time. Brick walls, stucco wings, and stone entrances give a house texture and warmth.

A *medieval window* is a casement window with small diamond-shaped panes of glass held together with lead strips.

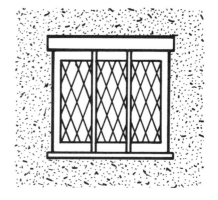

The Roman arch has a round semicircular head, the Gothic arch is pointed at the top, and the *Tudor arch* looks like a flattened Gothic arch.

NOTES

NOTES

CONTEMPORARY

ART DECO

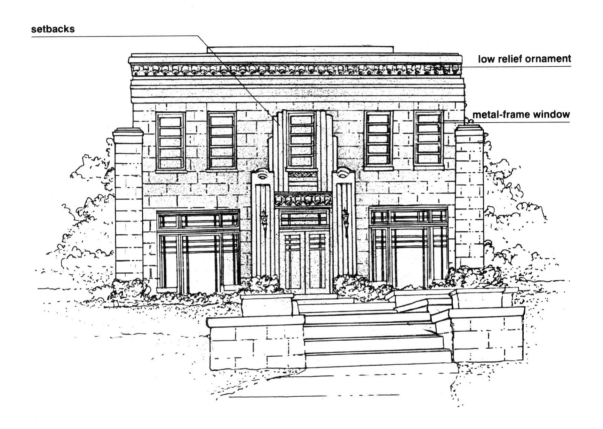

setbacks

low relief ornament

metal-frame window

At a Glance: These rectangular houses with smooth stucco walls and flat roofs feature a unique form of ornamentation. The front facade of an Art Deco style home uses a series of setbacks for vertical emphasis, beginning with a high central area and graduating to lower setbacks on each side. Low relief ornament is found around doors, windows, and roof. Typical motifs include zigzags, chevrons, and flowers, borrowing from such diverse sources as Egyptian and native American Indian art.

Background: The 1925 Exposition des Arts Decoratifs gave birth to the Art Deco movement. The ultimate expression of the style was in jewelry design, and Hollywood movies of the 1930s helped popularize Art Deco furnishings. The Art Deco style was employed in apartment buildings, office towers, theatres, and a few homes from the 1920s through the 1940s. Miami Beach, Florida, has a notable Art Deco district.

Focus on Features

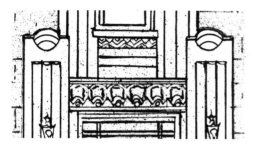

At the very root of the term *Art Deco* is the word *decoration*. The surface of an Art Deco building has a distinctive pattern of low relief designs carved into the smooth wall surface. Sharp linear angles create a zigzag of chevrons around the windows, doors, and cornice. A modified form of Art Deco style ornament was used on WPA (Work Projects Administration) buildings of the 1930s and 1940s.

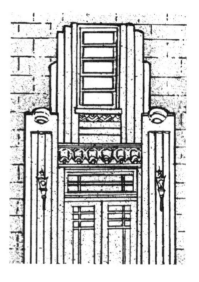

Most of the ornament focuses on the central area of the building and around the door. Here, the flat surface is molded into a series of setbacks, creating a step-like design.

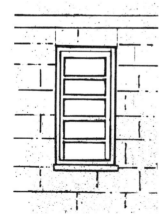

Windows in Art Deco buildings often have metal casements and railing instead of wood. These windows are likely to open outward on a hinge, rather than slide up and down within a frame as sash windows do.

ART MODERNE

glass blocks

flat roof

rounded edges

horizontal balustrade

slab door

At a Glance: Art Moderne houses have flat roofs and smooth walls rounded at the corners. Metal casement windows wrap building corners, and glass blocks provide ornament, especially around doors. A horizontal groove or band and a balustrade give a low emphasis to the streamlined appearance.

Background: Art Deco and Art Moderne styles are frequently confused. The key difference is that the Art Deco emphasizes the vertical with setbacks and sharp linear edges, while Art Moderne emphasizes the horizontal with rounded edges. The streamlined curve of the Art Moderne style was the favored industrial design of the 1930s, as is evident in the ships, cars, airplanes, and recreational vehicles of the era. It was popular for bus stations, apartments, and homes from about 1930 through the 1940s.

Focus on Features

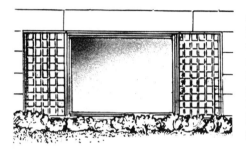

Glass blocks are a distinctive feature of Art Moderne buildings. They are like glass bricks, but hollow, and used only in non-load-bearing walls. Glass blocks admit light but maintain privacy, as it is difficult to see through their thick, often textured glass. While they do serve to insulate against noise, they are not good thermal insulators. Glass blocks were especially popular in the 1930s and 1940s when they were used around doors and windows and in bathrooms.

Nautical designs are another common characteristic of the Art Moderne style. Here, the metal roof railing around the balcony resembles the deck of an elegant cruise ship, and the front slab door has a portal window. In fact, industrial designs of both ships and cars influenced the architecture of the Art Moderne style. With their flat roofs, smooth walls, horizontal elements, and rounded surfaces, Art Moderne houses were said to look as though they were designed in a wind tunnel.

INTERNATIONAL

wrap-around
corner window

flat roof

recessed entrance

cantilevered
balcony

At a Glance: International style houses are plain boxes with multilevel flat roofs and walls of glass. They are the frank expression of skeleton construction. Using steel frame and/or reinforced concrete allows for non-supporting walls of glass and cantilevered projections.

Background: This avant-garde style reflected the European notion of the home as a "machine for living." The International style rejected the use of ornament to create historical associations. It has been popular primarily for architect-designed homes from 1940 through the 1990s.

Focus on Features

Architects of the International movement often employed a column at the foundation of a projection and cut back the base of the building to give it a suspended, gravity-defying appearance. Massive steel beams make it possible to extend or cantilever balconies horizontally without visible means of support.

Windows become more than windows in the International style; they become walls. Large areas of glass are grouped in horizontal bands to create a floating image. Windows often meet at the building's edge and, in effect, wrap around the corner.

Sliding glass doors are a common feature, and front doors are typically recessed. International style houses have smooth white surfaces, usually concrete or stucco, unburdened by applied ornament.

PRAIRIE

wide eaves

Craftsman column

ribbon window

French doors & sidelights

pedestal

At a Glance: The Prairie style employs every means possible to emphasize the horizontal. With wings spread out to each side and low hip roofs with wide overhangs, these massive brick structures seem to hug the ground. Squat columns support a deep, wide, one-story porch. Windows are grouped in horizontal bands, and even the bricks seem to be elongated.

Background: Prairie style houses (like Ranch style, which follows) are considered "contemporary" in that they are very much a product of the vision of Frank Lloyd Wright, who is considered the father of contemporary American architecture. Wright's philosophy was that a building should grow naturally from its site and harmonize with its surroundings; and the low, massive lines of the Prairie style were intended to harmonize with the level landscape and open sky of the Midwest. Though born in the plains, this style spread across America through plan books and magazines such as *Ladies' Home Journal*. It was popular from about 1900 through the 1920s, but was never as widely used as its spin-off, the Ranch style.

Focus on Features

When three or more windows are placed together, they are referred to as *ribbon windows*. Illustrated here are double-hung sash windows featuring a single pane in the bottom sash and several panes in the upper sash. These are called Craftsman windows and are typical of the architecture of the Arts and Crafts Movement. When these windows are grouped together, the divided upper sash creates a horizontal band across the facade.

A *French door* has small panes of glass throughout its entire length. Interior French doors were commonly used to separate the living room from the dining room in early-twentieth-century houses. Here, the front French door combined with the sidelights creates an entrance of glass. In the Prairie style, windows and doors were designed to admit as much light as possible. Magazines of the time touted the benefits of sunlight and fresh air, claiming that sunlight saved on doctor's bills.

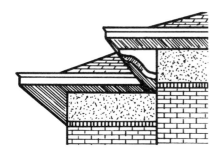

Several design devices are employed to emphasize the horizontal. The wide projecting eaves, for example, can make a tall building look low to the ground.

RANCH

picture window

carport

wrought iron columns

At a Glance: The standard Ranch style is a long, low brick house rambling and sprawling over a large grassy yard. These homes are the architectural expression of the American love affair with the automobile. A two-car garage is attached to the house, often facing the road. An imposing driveway with the mailbox at the street replaces the pedestrian sidewalk. Instead of a front or side porch, the backyard patio becomes the preferred open-air living space. Exterior detail is de-emphasized, though cast iron columns, decorative shutters, and picture windows are popular. Inside, ceilings are low and woodwork minimal.

Background: This style originated in California in the 1930s and was loosely based on the low, long Spanish Colonial ranches of the West. The Ranch is one of the most common American house styles. It reached the height of its popularity during the optimistic Eisenhower presidency and was still peaking in the 1970s.

Focus on Features

With the advent of the Ranch style, sheltered parking for the family car no longer required a separate outbuilding. A *carport*, open on three sides, was attached to the side of the house. It has been said that the two most important things to European men are food and wine, while the two most important things to American men are their cars and their home. The Ranch house perfectly justifies this maxim. The main entrance to the house is through the garage door and into the kitchen. This garage has a Colonial-looking *cupola* on top, which is both a decorative reminder of outbuildings of earlier times as well as a means of ventilation.

One distinctive feature of the Ranch style is the *picture window*, with its characteristic horizontal, three-part composition. The central section consists of one large, fixed pane of glass which provides an expansive "picture" of the scenery. This central window is flanked on each side by narrow sidelights, which often open and shut to allow for ventilation. The picture window, typically located in the living room, is often ornamented with shutters.

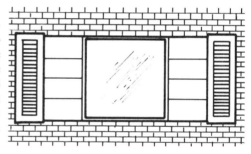

Lacy wrought iron and cast iron columns are popular supports for garages and entrances. Designs including grapes, flowers, ivy vines, and geometric shapes are incorporated into the mass-produced metal work. The use of iron columns is a subtle allusion to the Spanish origins of the Ranch style.

SPLIT-LEVEL

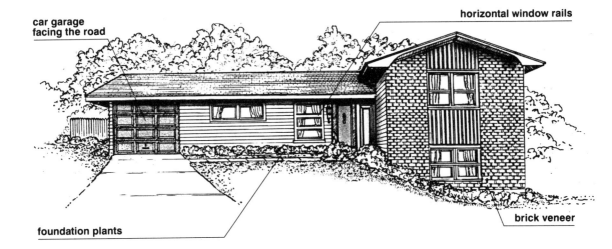

**car garage
facing the road**

horizontal window rails

brick veneer

foundation plants

At a Glance: The Split-Level is an innovative spin-off of the Ranch style. On the exterior it is similar to the Ranch, except that it has a two-story wing, and like the Ranch it is often brick or a brick-and-wood combination. On the interior, space is split into three levels: on the lowest level are the utility room and den; in the middle are the kitchen and living room; and upstairs are the bedrooms.

Background: This division of spaces is based on an academic theory that families function well in such discrete environments: service areas, noisy social spaces, quiet living areas, and a private sleeping area. The Split-Level was a favorite among speculative builders from 1950 through the 1970s.

Focus on Features

The long, low look popular in the Ranch and Split-Level is expressed in windows with *horizontal dividing rails*. The top of the windows typically runs directly under the eaves of the roof.

The open carport was soon followed by a garage enclosed on three sides and approached by a wide driveway with a mailbox at the end on the road. *Garage doors* became a decorative accent of garages that faced the street. The next step in this evolution was to move the entrance of the garage to the side or rear of the house, so that a brick wall and not an open garage faced passers-by.

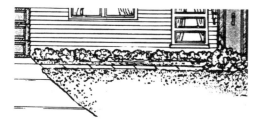

In the automobile suburbs, the walkway leads from the driveway to the front door, not from the street to the front door as it did when sidewalks were a common feature. Ornamental flowering shrubs and evergreens are typically planted at the foundation of the house. Large grassy front yards soon became a status symbol, and a rear patio became the outside social space for the family.

CONTEMPORARY RUSTIC

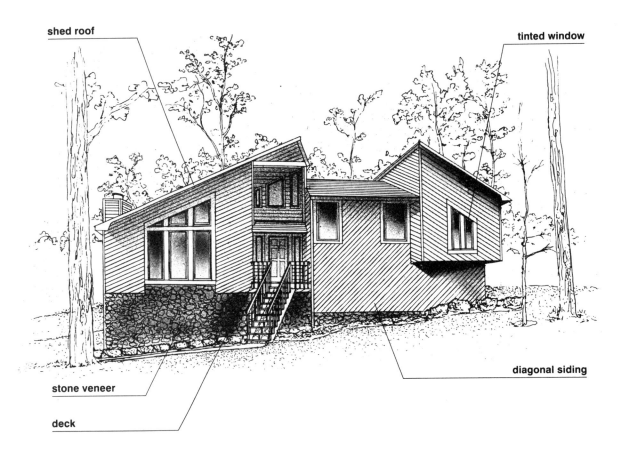

shed roof

tinted window

stone veneer

deck

diagonal siding

At a Glance: The most distinctive feature of the Contemporary Rustic style is the dramatic clash of angles in the roof. The basic roof shape is called the shed, which looks like the long slope of the Saltbox. This house style is typically clad with unpainted siding often set on the diagonal. Tinted windows in various geometric shapes are set asymmetrically into the walls. The entrance is recessed, and a deck is a common feature.

Background: This style is the architectural expression of the granola-and-earthshoes movement of the 1960s. The back-to-nature attitude is evident in the landscape, which is heavily forested and punctuated with ornamental boulders. The Contemporary Rustic style was born and bred in California and is often referred to as California Contemporary. It spread across the country in the late 1960s and 1970s.

Focus on Features

With its steeply pitched roofs colliding at various angles, the silhouette of the Contemporary Rustic style looks like a design conceived by a geometry professor gone mad. The most common roof component is called the *shed* — i.e., the single-slope roof commonly used for lean-to additions and storage buildings. Cedar shakes are often used as a roofing material. The dramatic angles of the roof suggest the soaring ceilings inside.

Instead of the traditional horizontal application of clapboard, the wood siding is nailed on the diagonal, with different walls having siding set at different angles. The exterior wood is often unpainted cedar, either stained or left in its natural state. Foundations and walls are often veneered with large stones.

Windows of the Contemporary Rustic style break with tradition in several ways. For example, their placement is varied; they can be found both high and low in the wall and even in the roof. Skylights in the roof and clerestory windows in the upper part of the wall also depart from orthodoxy. Windows are grouped into geometric compositions and come in various geometric shapes. They often have one large pane of tinted glass and open on a hinge if at all.

POST MODERN

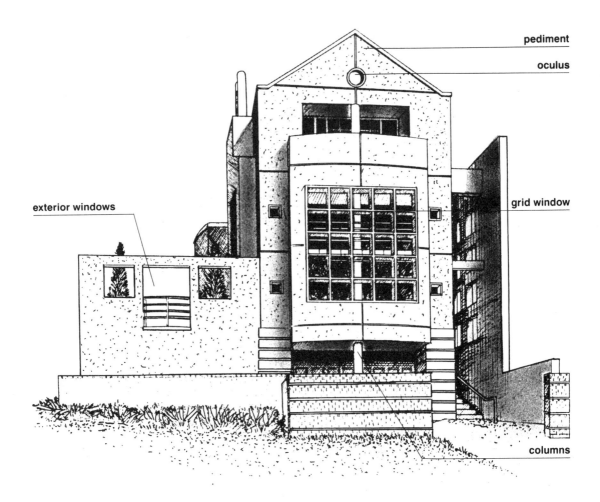

pediment

oculus

grid window

exterior windows

columns

At a Glance: Post Modern houses incorporate classical elements such as pediments, arched windows, and columns onto stucco or slick, smooth surfaces. Architects often designed these historical elements on a larger-than-life scale and combined them in a somewhat whimsical manner. Walls with window-like openings are used to define exterior space.

Background: Behind the slick facade of Post Modern architecture is a maze of complex intellectual theories. The style began as a reaction against the lack of ornament which had formed the basis of the modern architecture of the 1940s, 1950s, and 1960s. The Post Modern movement reached into the past to bring back classical elements, but used them on an exaggerated scale. The Post Modern style has been employed from the mid-1960s through the 1990s, though more often for shopping malls, office developments, and condominiums than for single family dwellings.

Focus on Features

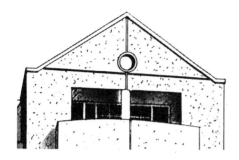

A typical feature of Post Modern houses is the triangular *pediment* with a circular window, or *oculus*. This design element is common in classical architecture and furniture.

Walls in Post Modern houses are used to define not only interior spaces but also exterior spaces such as gardens or patios. Balanced square openings in these exterior walls might frame a formal view of the garden, for example, and thus pay a historical debt to traditional walls. The surfaces of Post Modern buildings are smooth and often stark white, with pastel or primary colors defining accents.

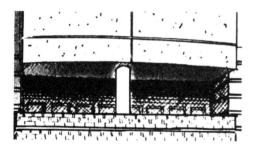

Sleek round columns are a typical feature of the style and are used in both a structural and decorative manner. Usually these columns are not crowned with classical *capitals*.

Large grids of windows cover the walls, flooding the spacious interiors with light.

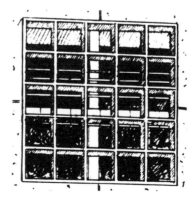

NOTES

NOTES

FAMILIAR AMERICAN

GABLED ELL

fishscale shingles

Queen Anne window

wrap-around porch

At a Glance: The Gabled Ell, not surprisingly, has a distinctive "L" shape. This one- or two-story frame house has a gable roof and two wings, creating a front gable and a side gable. One-story porches with shed or hipped roofs are common. Gabled ells can be quite simple or very decorative. Typically they are sheathed with clapboard.

Background: The Gabled Ell was a common house style, especially in small towns, from about 1880 to 1910. Local carpenters often embellished this basic design with bargeboards, brackets, shingles, and gingerbread, creating houses with various stylistic elements. Most mail-order companies claimed that Gabled Ells were among their best sellers because they were conservative and economical.

Focus on Features

Gables were a primary target for decoration in these basic L-shaped houses. Shingles of various shapes placed in the gable created an interesting texture. One of the most common types was the *fishscale shingle*, so named because the end of the shingle was rounded to look like scales of a fish. Other common shingles had square or pointed ends.

A *Queen Anne window* is easy to recognize: it has one large pane of glass surrounded by smaller blocks of stained glass. This window was a common stock item around the turn of the century and was often placed in front doors. *Stained glass* became a popular way to introduce color and yet maintain privacy in the Victorian Era. Stained glass windows were commonly placed at the landing of a staircase, in the parlor or dining room, and around the front door.

TEMPLE FRONT

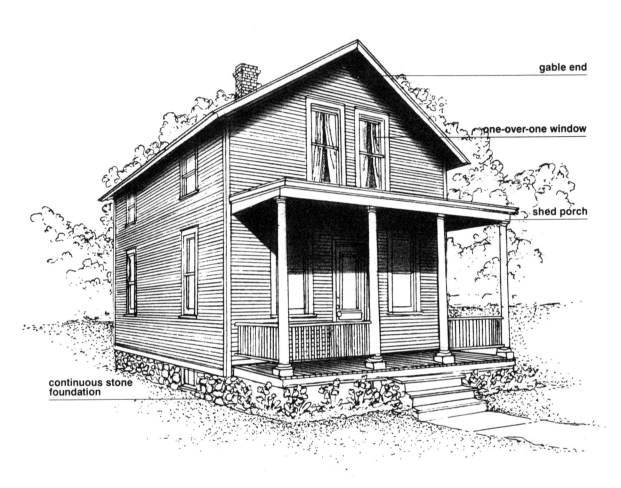

gable end

one-over-one window

shed porch

continuous stone
foundation

At a Glance: The Temple Front house is a two-story dwelling with an open gable form facing the road. It usually has a one-story porch, a side entrance, and a side hall. Onto this basic form any number of stylistic elements were added to give the house a Victorian or classical look.

Background: The style is named *Temple Front* because the gable opens toward the road like that of a Greek temple. The Temple Front was a common urban style from 1880 to the 1920s, when it was a popular mail-order, pre-fabricated plan. Aladdin and Company from Bay City, Michigan, sold a pre-cut, ready-to-assemble Temple Front house called the "Carolina" for $1,954 in 1919.

Focus on Features

As noted earlier, windows can provide a clue to the date of a building's construction. Early glass panes were blown from molten glass, so the surfaces are wavy and the panes are small. In general, the smaller the panes and the larger the number of panes in the windows, the earlier the house. For example, Colonial houses built during the 1700s often have as many as twelve panes of glass in each sash. By the 1830s, it was more common to have nine-over-nine windows or six-over-six. By 1880, new glass-making technology made it possible to create large windows with a single pane of glass. Additives were mixed with the molten glass which allowed it to be rolled out into large sheets. One-over-one windows indicate that a house was probably built around 1880 or later. When this new technology was applied to commercial building, the result was plate-glass storefronts.

Around 1900, *continuous foundations* began to replace open-pier foundations. Continuous foundations provided shelter for plumbing, as well as an enclosed space for storage. A chute on the side allowed coal to be dropped into the storage area in the basement, where it was used as fuel for the furnace. One factor which may have encouraged the switch away from coal heating was the prolonged miners' strike in 1946. John Lewis, the leader of the miners, became a household name when Americans began to run out of coal. Heating contractors hurriedly installed gas furnaces to satisfy the countless homeowners who called to "get John Lewis out of my basement."

SHOTGUN

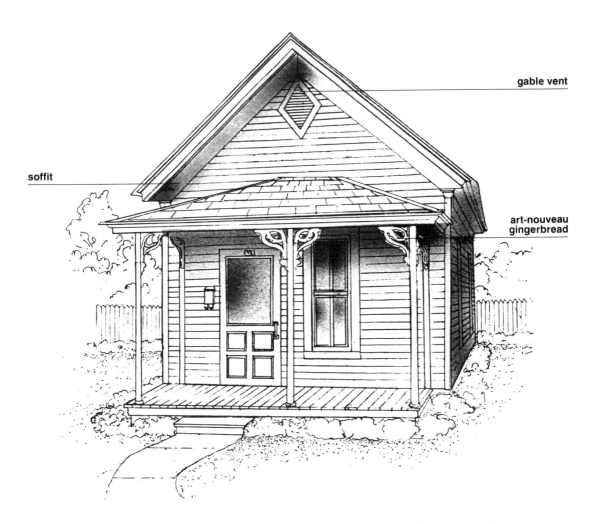

gable vent

soffit

art-nouveau
gingerbread

At a Glance: The unmistakable Shotgun house is long and narrow. It is one story high, one room wide, and several rooms long, with the gable end of the roof facing the road. Double-Shotgun houses follow a similar pattern, but have double the width and two front doors.

Background: The name *Shotgun* supposedly comes from the theory that if you stand at the front door and shoot a gun straight through the house, the bullet will come out the back door. Sears, Roebuck advertised that their Shotgun house, which sold for $210 in 1911, could be built in twenty-four hours. Architectural historians have traced the origin of the Shotgun house back to early-nineteenth-century New Orleans, where it developed from African, French, and American Indian traditions. In the South especially, these houses proliferated in industrial mill towns and Black neighborhoods from 1880 through the 1910s.

Focus on Features

The *gable roof* is one of the most common roof types in America. It consists of a ridge with a slope to each side, with the gable end creating a triangular shape. In the Shotgun house the gable end faces the road. Inside the gable is a diamond-shaped gable vent, which allows for the flow of air through the roof.

Shotgun houses almost always have a one-story front porch, which not only serves as an entrance but also creates an important outdoor living space for this small dwelling. The design of these gingerbread column brackets is *art nouveau*, a style of decoration developed in France at the end of the nineteenth century. It is characterized by flowing lines and curving organic shapes.

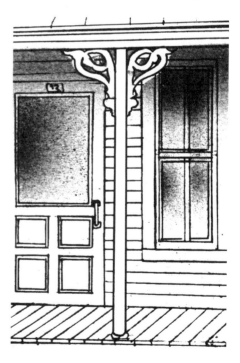

VERNACULAR FARMHOUSE

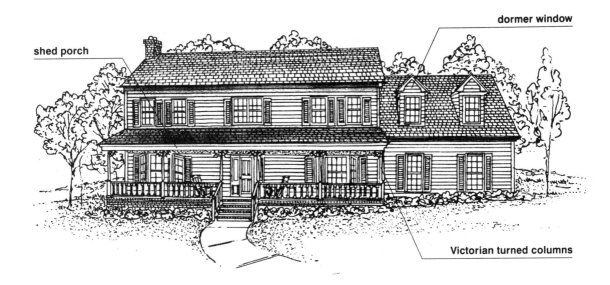

shed porch

dormer window

Victorian turned columns

At a Glance: Vernacular Farmhouses are informal, rambling, two-story frame houses with one-story front porches. Gable roofs and dormer windows are common. Colonial and Victorian features are often mixed.

Background: When the term *vernacular* is applied to language, it refers to a local dialect; when it applies to architecture, it refers to the use of regional forms and materials. Vernacular homes are often identified by their structure, rather than ornament. When ornament is applied, it is a local interpretation of national or international styles. As the rural farm family became a vestige of a vanishing way of life, suburban homes in the late-twentieth century sought to recreate the homey feel of the country farmhouse.

Focus on Features

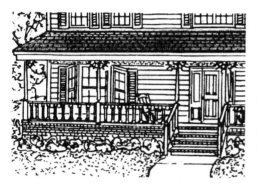

The Vernacular Farmhouse can be seen as an attempt to return to the good old days, with a rocking chair on the front porch of an informal, rambling country home. Colonial windows combine with Victorian turned porch columns to create an idealized vision of the American farmhouse. Ornamental details are borrowed from different eras to make the house look as though it has been added onto over time.

Garages are designed to look like additions to the original house or like old-fashioned outbuildings.

I-HOUSE

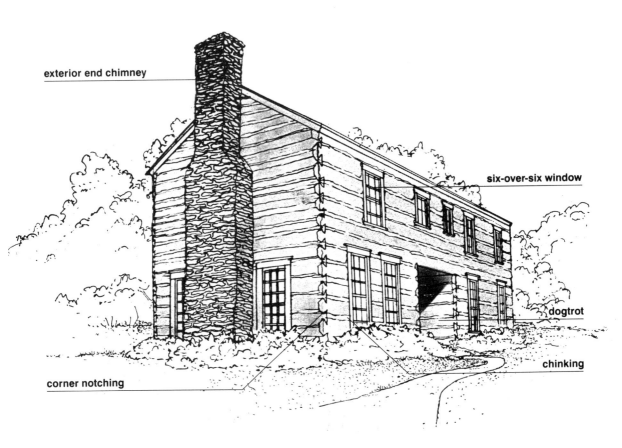

exterior end chimney

six-over-six window

dogtrot

chinking

corner notching

At a Glance: The I-house is two stories high and one room deep. This tall, distinctive style has at least two rooms on each floor. It can be constructed of stone, logs, bricks, or wood frame. I-houses typically have a gable roof, exterior end chimneys, and one-story front and rear porches.

Background: The term *I-house* was coined in the 1960s by folk geographers who had undertaken to survey vernacular buildings in several midwestern states, all of which coincidentally began with the letter "I." The geographers found this to be a common house type, two stories tall and one room deep, and so called it the "I"-house. In fact, however, the I-house is common not only in the Midwest but throughout the country and was popular from Colonial times through the early-twentieth century. Some I-houses are very plain; others have been embellished with classical and Victorian elements.

Focus on Features

The opening in the middle of the house is called a *dogtrot* or *possum-trot* because animals could roam through it freely. The dogtrot was especially suited to a warm climate where it functioned as a breezeway and created a cool living space.

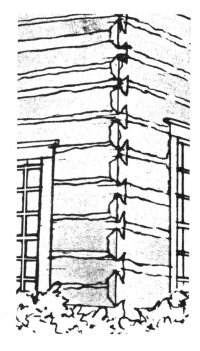

Log cabins seem as American as apple pie. At least seven of our presidents were born or lived in one. But folk geographers trace American log construction back to immigrants from northern European countries such as Sweden and Finland, where building with horizontal logs had long been a tradition. Log walls are joined at the corner by *corner notching*, in which the corners of logs are shaped to fit together like a handshake. Notching types are named for their shape: dovetail, saddlebag, or square. The gaps between the logs were filled with *chinking* made from clay, mud, rock, or leaves. Chinking was often seasonal — removed in the summer to allow for light and ventilation, then replaced in the fall to keep the house warm in the winter.

CRAFTSMAN BUNGALOW

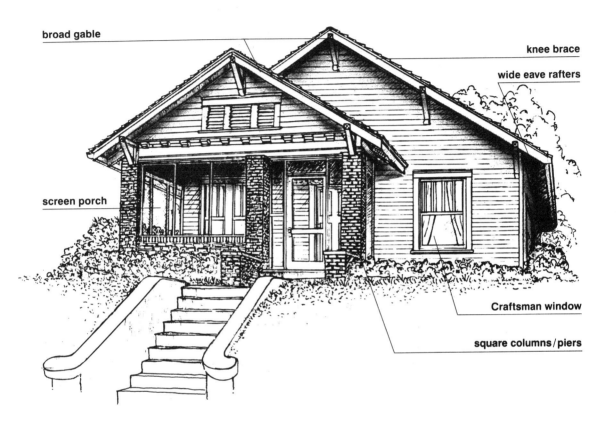

broad gable

knee brace

wide eave rafters

screen porch

Craftsman window

square columns/piers

At a Glance: Craftsman style homes have low gable or hip roofs with a wide overhang. Structural roof supports such as knee braces and rafters are exposed. Wide, deep front porches are supported by thick, square, simple columns which often sit on brick or stone pedestals. Windows are frequently grouped in pairs or ribbons. One- or one-and-a-half-story Craftsman houses are called *bungalows*.

Background: The Craftsman (or Arts and Crafts) Movement in America developed as a reaction against the machine-made ornamental excess of the Victorian era. This was a back-to-nature movement, reflecting a desire to return to simpler times when craftsmen worked with their hands and took pride in detail. In architecture, structural detail and the use of good materials were prized over applied ornamentation. The bungalow has its roots in California, where this style was well suited to the warm climate. It then spread across the country to become one of the most common middle-class house designs from 1910 to the 1930s.

Focus on Features

The term *bungalow* comes to us from India, where low houses with wide roofs and deep porches were common in Bengal. Our word is a British corruption of the Hindu adjective meaning "belonging to Bengal." The front-gable bungalow seen here with two broad overlapping gables is one of the most common styles.

Wire-mesh screen was used on windows and doors in the Victorian era, but it was the Craftsman style that introduced the *screen porch* to the American home. Screen porches served to blur the distinction between outside and interior space and allowed the benefits of fresh air to be enjoyed without the annoyance of insects.

The distinctive *Craftsman window* has a single pane of glass in the lower sash and several panes in the upper sash.

SIDE-GABLE BUNGALOW

rafters

central dormer

knee brace

wide eaves

pedestal

battered columns

At a Glance: The relation between the gable and the road tells us whether to call a bungalow "front-gable" or "side-gable." On the side-gable bungalow, the long slope of the roof sweeping down the front of the house creates a wide, deep front porch. There is usually one central dormer.

Background: Gustav Stickley, a furniture designer, became the father of the American Arts and Crafts Movement. His magazine, *Craftsman*, and others like it provided working drawings for these houses. The bungalow styles came to epitomize the American dream in that they were easily mass-produced and affordable.

Focus on Features

Massive, thick porch columns such as these are a typical feature of Craftsman bungalows. Tapered columns, thicker at the base than at the top, are called *battered columns*. The short, thick piers to each side of the entrance stairs are called *pedestals*. When the sweeping lines of the roof cover the front porch, it is called an *engaged porch*.

The large central dormer window is a common feature of side-gable bungalows. Like the main roof, the roof of the dormer has wide eaves with exposed rafters and triangular supports called *knee braces*.

A large exterior chimney was often included in the Craftsman design. One wall of the living room typically featured a low, long, simple brick mantel with built-in bookshelves to each side. In the first decades of the twentieth century, when hot-air furnaces assumed the role previously assigned to the fireplace, fireplaces took on a symbolic role as the center of happy family life.

Another Craftsman touch was built-in furniture such as buffets and windows seats, which were promoted in magazines of the early-twentieth century as making a house easy to clean. One magazine noted that the housewife of the future will say that the ideal home is one that can be cleaned with a hose.

HIPPED BUNGALOW

Craftsman column

hip roof

vestibule door

closed railing

At a Glance: The tall hip roof is the distinguishing feature of the hipped bungalow. These boxy houses are covered with clapboard or shingles, and one-story front porches are common.

Background: This house style was common in the South, Midwest, and West from about 1870 to the 1930s. Early versions have Victorian details, while later ones display Craftsman features. Several mail-order companies sold pre-cut hipped bungalows, suitable for housing workers in factory towns.

Focus on Features

The hip roof was particularly appropriate for hot climates, since warm air would rise up into the high roof and leave the rooms below cooler. Three-sided hip roofs where the slopes meet at a point are called *pyramidal roofs*, so named because the shape looks like an Egyptian pyramid.

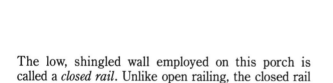

The low, shingled wall employed on this porch is called a *closed rail*. Unlike open railing, the closed rail clearly defines the boundary between outside and inside space.

AMERICAN FOURSQUARE

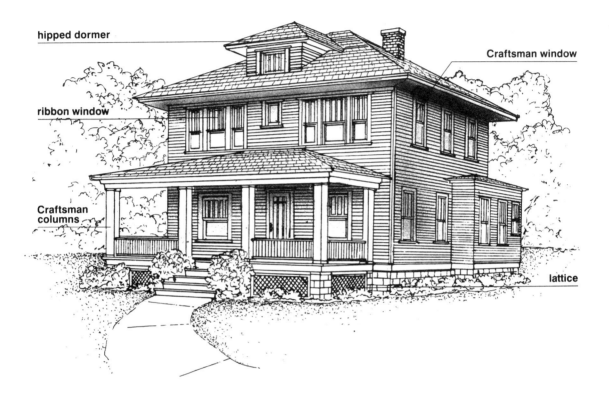

hipped dormer

Craftsman window

ribbon window

Craftsman columns

lattice

At a Glance: A wide hip roof, often containing a central hipped dormer, gives a massive quality to the boxy shape of this two-story house. The one-story verandah spans the front of the house and is approached by several steps. Most Foursquares were built of wood, but brick and concrete blocks were also common building materials. Some have shingles on the second story and clapboard on the first. Windows are often grouped or paired, and a bay window commonly projects from one side of the house.

Background: Examples of American Foursquare can be found in almost every American community. An economical and practical house to build, the Foursquare was popular from about 1900 through the 1930s. Most mail-order house companies sold several versions of the style, and one 1919 catalog offered all the materials for a Foursquare for $2,529. The catalog described the house as "truly American—simple, strong, and substantial," and its interior arrangement was given a stamp of approval by housewives for being "convenient and comfortable, minimizing housework." This popular post-Victorian house has been called the American Foursquare because the square shape of the two-story house could accommodate four equal-sized rooms on each floor.

Focus on Features

The *central hipped dormer* is a common feature of the American Foursquare. This low, wide dormer admits light into the attic area, which is used for storage or made into bedrooms. Rooms in the attic were often provided for domestic helpers, who assisted the middle- and upper-class housewives with daily chores.

The overall shape and massive solid quality of the Foursquare differ greatly from the asymmetrical shapes and fanciful ornamentation of the Victorian homes that were so popular just prior to the twentieth century. The front porch vividly illustrates the difference between the two styles. Though the porch is still an important feature, gone are the gingerbread, the turned columns, and the balusters of the Victorian home. Instead, Foursquares have deep, one-story porches supported by three or four thick, simple columns which often sit on piers of brick or stone. Railings also tend to be square and simple. Several steps lead up to the porch of the Foursquare, which is elevated off the ground on piers. Often lattice panels are placed between the piers to prevent animals from crawling under the house.

NOTES

NOTES

PICTORIAL GLOSSARY

WINDOWS

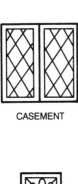

CASEMENT

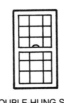

DOUBLE-HUNG SASH

TRIPLE-HUNG SASH

QUEEN ANNE

COTTAGE

CRAFTSMAN

TWO-OVER-TWO

ROMAN OR ROUNDED ARCH

PALLADIAN

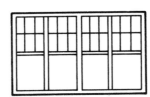

RIBBON

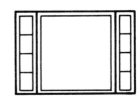

PICTURE

ONE-OVER-ONE

GOTHIC

TRI-PART

CRAFTSMAN

ENTRANCES

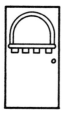

CRAFTSMAN

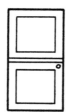

DUTCH

FOUR-PANEL

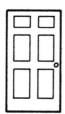

SIX PANEL/CROSS & OPEN BIBLE

VESTIBULE

FANLIGHT

PEDIMENTED

BROKEN PEDIMENT

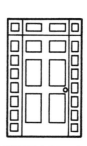

TRANSOM & SIDELIGHT

PORCHES

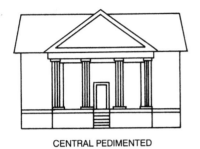

CENTRAL PEDIMENTED

INSET

TWO-TIER

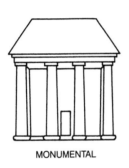

MONUMENTAL

WRAP-AROUND

SIDE

SHED

ENTRANCE STOOP

CRAFTSMAN

MATERIALS

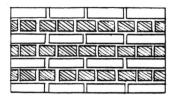

ENGLISH BOND

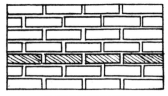

STRETCHER BOND

STRETCHER

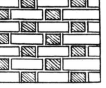

FLEMISH BOND

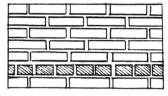

COMMON BOND

HEADER

SOLDIER

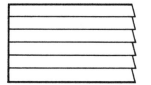

CLAPBOARD OR WEATHERBOARD

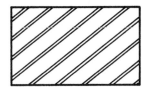

DIAGONAL SIDING

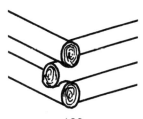

LOG

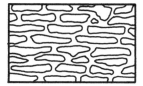

FIELDSTONE

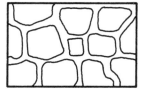

RANDOM COURSED STONE

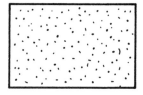

STUCCO

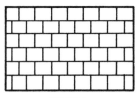

SHINGLE

ROOFS

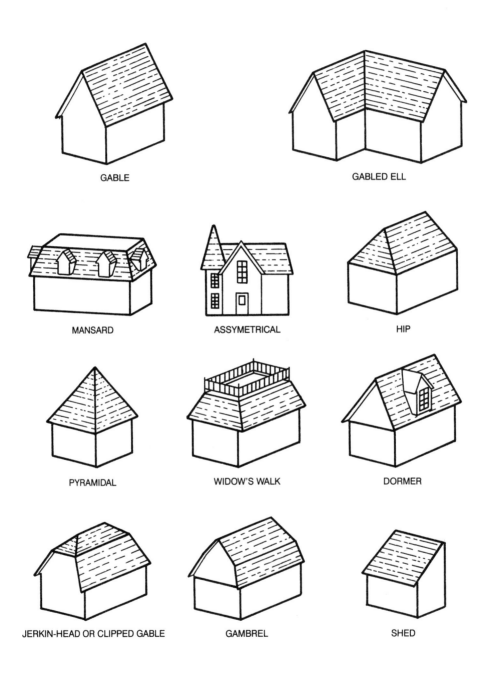

GABLE

GABLED ELL

MANSARD

ASSYMETRICAL

HIP

PYRAMIDAL

WIDOW'S WALK

DORMER

JERKIN-HEAD OR CLIPPED GABLE

GAMBREL

SHED

DETAILS

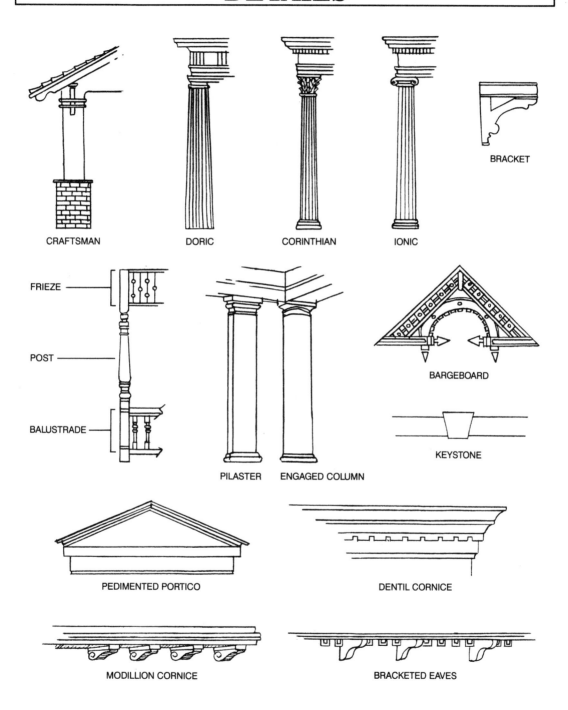

CRAFTSMAN

DORIC

CORINTHIAN

IONIC

BRACKET

FRIEZE

POST

BALUSTRADE

PILASTER   ENGAGED COLUMN

BARGEBOARD

KEYSTONE

PEDIMENTED PORTICO

DENTIL CORNICE

MODILLION CORNICE

BRACKETED EAVES

NOTES

NOTES

INDEX

NOTES

NOTES

NOTES

NOTES